T0103628

Lifecycle Gates in a Christian's Life

Nehemiah 3—Gates in a Christian's Life

Elizabeth Washington

WESTBOW·
PRESS
A DIVISION OF THOMAS NELSON
& ZONDERVAN

Copyright © 2015 Elizabeth Washington.

All rights reserved. No part of this book may be used or reproduced by
any means, graphic, electronic, or mechanical, including photocopying,
recording, taping or by any information storage retrieval system
without the written permission of the publisher except in the case
of brief quotations embodied in critical articles and reviews.

Scripture taken from the King James Version of the Bible.

WestBow Press books may be ordered through booksellers or by contacting:

WestBow Press
A Division of Thomas Nelson & Zondervan
1663 Liberty Drive
Bloomington, IN 47403
www.westbowpress.com
1 (866) 928-1240

Because of the dynamic nature of the Internet, any web addresses or
links contained in this book may have changed since publication and
may no longer be valid. The views expressed in this work are solely those
of the author and do not necessarily reflect the views of the publisher,
and the publisher hereby disclaims any responsibility for them.

Any people depicted in stock imagery provided by Thinkstock are
models, and such images are being used for illustrative purposes only.
Certain stock imagery © Thinkstock.

ISBN: 978-1-4908-7061-8 (sc)
ISBN: 978-1-4908-7062-5 (e)

Library of Congress Control Number: 2015902682

Print information available on the last page.

WestBow Press rev. date: 03/26/2015

Contents

Introduction

Life contains a sequence of events that helps to shape your destination of success or failure as a Christian. Everyone who is alive will go through the lifespan gates of life from birth to death, 1 to 120 years the life span given by God, **Genesis 6:3** – And the Lord said, My spirit shall not always strive with man, for that he also is flesh: yet his days shall be an hundred and twenty years. Everyone has a time appointed by God, **Ecclesiastes 3:2** – A time to be born, and a time to die. This book will address the "Lifecycle Gate" in a Christian's life which will develops, matures and gives growth as you walk with the Lord. As you walk with the Lord, these gates are rewarding and beneficial and worthy to be associated with the various gates mentioned in **Nehemiah 3**. Once you have accepted the Lord into your life as your personal Saviour, your day of salvation, you will have to walk through all these gates in a series of actions directed with a specific aim. This aim is to take you from earth to reside eternally in heaven. You may have to walk through different gates two or three times to sustain your daily walk, growth and preserve wisdom. These gates are not to break you but to make you a more confident child of God and give you a testimony. Testimony is what the Lord has done for you through the good times and the bad times. Always remember, satan is there to meet you at each gate. He will even walk in with you, take his seat and try to make you fail. You must make satan uncomfortable by worshipping God and praising God and this will make satan feel very uncomfortable. Surround yourself in the Word of God and know that "It is Written" to help you to maintain your spiritual walk with the Lord. Most of all always remember and know the Lord is present in every gate. Jesus is your omnipresent God. Each gate holds a new learning encounter that helps you to walk differently than the society around you, **Galatians 5:25** – If we live in the Spirit, let us also walk in the Spirit. Each gate will bring you closer and closer to your Lord. You will be branded as strange or peculiar, but remember the Lord called you peculiar first and chose you, **I Peter 2:9** – But ye are a chosen generation, a royal priesthood, an holy nation, a peculiar people; that ye should shew forth the praises of him who hath called you out of darkness into his marvelous light. Each gate is an experience to show forth in your life to others what the Lord has done for you because of that particular gate's experience. In each gate you will grow in the love of God and get to know your own strength to love or tolerate people. You will tell others what God can do because of your gate experience and relate to others what God can't do because God can do all things but fail. The church calls this a "Testimony." In each gate there is a "test" to give you a "testimony." Time spent in each gate will differ between yourself and another person because we all have different personalities in God but we all must have the same mind, **Romans 12:2** - And be not conformed to this world: but be ye transformed by the renewing of our mind, that ye may prove what is that good, and acceptable, and perfect, will of God. Each gate will teach you what is good for you, what is acceptable and the perfect will of God for your life. You will know that God is "Real". You will know how rewarding it is to serve the True and Living God of the Bible, **Romans 1:20** – For the invisible things of him from the creation of the world are clearly seen, being understood by the things that are made, even his eternal power and Godhead; so that they are without excuse. In each gate there is no fakeness because we serve a God that cannot lie; the Lord is the God of truth. Enter into each gate with thanksgiving and recognize the gate as the gate that the righteous shall enter, **Psalm 118:20** and you are the righteousness of God in each gate. Enter into each gate, read and look at yourself because each gate helps you to prepare for the next gate and most of all they prepare you for the coming of the Lord. When you pass through a gate and there is question in your heart why did you end up in that particular gate, you will not proceed until you find the answer. Questions deserve an answer and each answer will come from the Word of God. You will graduate from each gate when you get the answer given by the Spirit of God. You will not proceed further until you find the truth, the answer from the Lord. You will always have a gate to go through in your life with your walk with the Lord. Each gate will help you to keep going to the end with endurance, joy, peace, and faith in God. It is time to return back to the Author and the Finisher of our faith, look to Him because He endured the Cross of Calvary for you and took the shame of sin for the world, **Hebrews 12:2** – Looking unto Jesus the author and finisher of our faith; who for the joy that was set before him endured the cross, despising the shame, and is set down at the right hand of the throne of God. This is why it is such a great joy to walk through the each gate and see the welcome mat set down by the Lord. On that day, the Lord will welcome you because you have accepted the Lord's direction while proceeding through each gate. Through each gate you will begin to recognize and know Jesus by the fellowship of His suffering, **Philippines 3:10** – That I may know him, and the power of his resurrection, and the fellowship of his suffering, being made conformable unto his death, and know God through Jesus by the power of the Holy Ghost. A gate is just an entrance, an opening and Jesus who is the door of life and in each gate, you just entered where Jesus wants you to be, **John 10:9** – I am the door: by me if any man enters in, he shall be saved, and shall go in and out, and find pasture. Continue to hold on to your faith and don't give up on God. Deny the works of satan in your life and everywhere you go because wherever you are, you will be in a gate. Jesus is the One who walks with you through every opening, gate, in your Christian life. No matter what gate you are sitting in right now, be content and enjoy your temporary reside. In each gate, remember, the God of the Bible, your God is omnipotent, omnipresent, and omniscient and has Holy Ghost power working in you and through you. The Sheep Gate is a permanent gate which you must call home. You are at peace with your Creator, God. Love your position in time and you will appreciate each gate as you learn striving with determination toward eternity. In each gate you must remember always your experience in the Sheep Gate and you belong to the Good Shepherd, Jesus Christ. In each gate, you must keep in touch with Jesus by keeping Him your mind and He will provide you instructions, guidance in His love for favor, grace and mercy in each gate. Jesus will never fail you because you are saved by His amazing grace. First Gate, the Sheep Gate, is the gate that opens your entrance to the other gates. Prepare your life for the journey through obedience to the Word of God because it is only the Word of God that will deliver you while you reside in each gate. Enjoy the adventure set before you on your lifecycle journey from earth to heaven. Welcome to the first gate, the acceptance gate, the Sheep Gate.

1

Sheep's Gate – Nehemiah 3:1, 32

Yes, the Sheep Gate is the first and the only first gate that you must come in and make your permanent residence because of the love of God. In the Sheep Gate you begin to live again to live eternally. The Sheep Gate is known as the "Love" Gate because the True and Living God has appeared unto you and called you to come unto Him, **Jeremiah 31:3** – The Lord hath appeared of old unto me, saying, Yea, I have loved thee with an everlasting love: therefore with loving-kindness have I drawn thee. You can never say that you found the Lord but that the Lord found you. You were the one that was lost and in darkness. Jesus is never lost and is never in darkness. Jesus is the Light of the world. In the Sheep Gate, the Lord found you first and directed you toward the gate because you found and looked upon Him and believed Him for a new life for salvation, **John 5:24** – Verily, verily, I say unto you, He that hearth my word, and believeth on him that sent me, hath everlasting life, and shall not come into condemnation; but is passed from death unto life. You were predestinated to be saved from the foundation of the earth. God saw you just where you were and came to see about His predestinated child because of His Son, Jesus Christ, **Ephesian 1:3-4** – Blessed be the God and Father of our Lord Jesus Christ, who hath blessed us with all spiritual blessings in heavenly places in Christ: According as he hath chosen us in him before the foundation of the world, that we should be holy and without blame before him in love. You have accepted the Lord into your life and you are now in right standing with God, holy, blameless and loved by the Lord. You are now the responsibility of The Lord. Just trust in the love of the Lord from your introduction to the Sheep's Gate on the earth to the wind-up as you walk toward heaven's Final Gate. The Sheep Gate is the gate of "Salvation." Salvation means "Deliverance." You will be like Nicodemus and come to the conclusion that you must be born again, **John 3:7**. You had a personal encounter with the Savior of the World and this gate opened wide because of the Cross of Calvary. Jesus' arms were stretched wide welcoming you and the whole world because He was dying for your the sins, **John 3:16** – For God so loved the world, that he gave his only begotten Son, that whosoever believeth in him, should not perish, but have everlasting life. All because of two words, "Forgive", **Luke 23:34** – Then said Jesus, Father, forgive them; for they know not what they do and "Finished", **John 19:30** – When Jesus therefore had received the vinegar, he said, It is finished: and he bowed his head, and gave up the ghost. The gate is opened wide just for you to come inside. There is no fear. The perfect love of God cast out all fear. The love of God is waiting for you here in the Sheep Gate because you have accepted the Lord and the Lord has accepted you and now is your Shepherd, **Psalm 23:1**. The weight of sin and shame has been forgiven and washed away by the blood of Jesus. Your sins are forgiven. You will learn as you walk through the Word of God that Jesus is the Good Shepherd, **John 10:14**. You will begin to get acquainted with the Lord because He has always been acquainted with you from your mother's womb, **Jeremiah 1:5** and you had been set apart for the Master's use, **Galatians 1:15** – But when it pleased God, who separated me from my mother's womb, and called me by his grace. In the Sheep Gate, you will begin to know and try Jesus for yourself. Many say that mother knew Jesus and your dad may have known Jesus, but now you know Jesus. In the Sheep's Gate you are introduced to the shepherd of your soul, Jesus, **John 10:11** – I am the good shepherd; the good shepherd giveth his life for the sheep. The Shepherd of your soul has made you His responsibility by giving His life and dying on the Cross of Calvary. As you stroll through the gate, your mind will reflect on the Easter story and you will remember Calvary. Jesus died for the sins of the world that you can be saved, **Romans 11:26-27** – And so all Israel shall be saved: as it is written, There shall come out of Sion the Deliverer, and shall turn away ungodliness from Jacob: For this is my covenant unto them, when I shall take away their sins. Jesus knows more about you than you know about yourself and is mindful of you, **Psalm 8:4-6** – What is man, that thou art mindful of him? And the son of man, that thou visits him? For thou hast made him a little lower than the angels, and hast crowned him with glory and honor. Thou made him to have dominion over the works of thy hands; thou hast put all things under his feet. The Lord is sympathetic of all things concerning you once you are in the Sheep Gate. Just love the Lord and walk humbly with the Lord and no good thing will He withhold from you because you walk upright before Him, **Psalms 84:11** – For the Lord God is a sun and shield: the Lord will give grace and glory: no good thing will he withhold from them that walk uprightly. You must always remember in the Sheep's Gate, the Lord found you and He will never leave you alone. **II Thessalonians 3:3** – But the Lord is faithful, who shall stablish you, and keep you from evil. Put your trust in the faithfulness of your God. You heard His Voice calling you into the Sheep's Gate, **John 10:27** – My sheep hear my voice, and I know them, and they follow me. Old friends, worldly friends, will turn away because of your relationship with the Lord. They were not there when you heard the Voice of the Lord speaking to you. You will be like Paul, no man heard or seen what Paul heard and saw. He called you out of the world of sin. What an honor, the Lord knew you before you knew Him. This is worthy, **Ephesian 1:4**, to be mentioned again. The most honorable thing about the call of God, the call was from the very foundation of the world, **Ephesian 1:4** – According as he hath chosen us in him before the foundation of the world, that we should be holy and without blame before him in love: having predestinated us unto the adoption of children by Jesus Christ to himself, according to the good pleasure of his will, to the praise of the glory of his grace, wherein he hath made us accepted in the beloved. You are loved by God and adopted into the family of God. You were a lost sheep with no hope or direction in life but now you have cross over into the Sheep's Gate and you have come out of the world and the Lord is praying for you because God has given you to Him, **John 17:9** – I pray for them: I pray not for the word, but for them which thou hast given me; for they are thine. You heard the Voice of the Father, God, and now have accepted the Lord as your personal Savior by confessing your sins, **II Corinthians 7:10** – For godly sorrow worked repentance to salvation not to be repented of: for the sorrow of the world worked death. With heart broken and tears flowing, you have asked the Lord to forgive you of your sins and now you have become a partaker of this great salvation and you are now a believer in Jesus Christ, **Romans 10:9-10** – That if thou shalt confess with thy mouth the Lord Jesus, and shalt believe in thine heart that God hath raised him from the dead, thou shalt be saved. For with the heart man believeth unto righteousness, and with the mouth confession is made unto salvation. You have renounced sin, accepted the Lord into your heart, forgiven of your sins, accepted by God and now you are "Saved", delivered from the world of sin. As you travel to the other gates in the Christian life, you must stay strong and fear not and it is ok to be afraid but keep traveling because the Lord will never fail you, **Deuteronomy 31:6** – Be strong and of a good courage, fear not, nor be afraid or them: for the Lord thy God, he it is that doth go with thee; he will not fail thee, nor forsake thee. Now, breathe this fresh air of the newness of life in God and begin to walk with the Lord. You are now a new creature in Christ Jesus, **II Corinthians 5:17** and old things have passed away. The works of the flesh which is the old life of sin is gone, **Galatians 6:19-21** – Now the works of the flesh are manifest, which are these; Adultery, fornication, uncleanness, lasciviousness, idolatry, witchcraft, hatred, variance, emulations, wrath, strife, seditions, heresies, envying, murders, drunkenness, retellings, and such like, all things that all unrighteous. Sin(s) is the making of unrighteousness and will not allow you to enter into one of the twelve gates in heaven, and remember, **I John 5:17** – All unrighteousness is sin and they which do such things shall not inherit the kingdom of God. You do not walk as children of disobedience or a child of darkness, **Ephesians 2:2** – Wherein in time past ye walked according to the course of this world, according to the prince of the power of the air, the spirit that now worked in the children of disobedience. Satan lost a soul that he thought he owned. The Lord will teach you His ways that are not your ways and lead you in a straight path, **Psalm 143:10**. Always remember that you have been chosen to come into the Sheep Gate, stay peculiar, **I Peter 2:9** – But ye are a chosen generation, a royal priesthood, an holy nation, a peculiar people; that ye should shew forth the praises of him who hath called you out of darkness into his marvelous light. Stay a humble sheep in each gate to be exalted by the Lord with more joy and peace, **I Peter 5:6**, and talk to the Lord, in prayer. The most important aspect as a sheep is to grow in the Lord according to the Word of God, the Bible, daily, **II Peter 3:18** – But grow in grace, and in the knowledge of our Lord and Savior Jesus Christ. Amen. Amen means in the sheep, you agree in all the directions given to you by the Word of God. Each morning when you arise, you are thankful to Jesus for another day and tell and show the Lord how much you love Him. The best part of the Sheep Gate is accepting the Lord that brings redemption into your life, **Matthew 11:28**, but the worst part of the Sheep Gate is rejection of this great salvation by walking contrary to the Word of God in the Sheep Gate. As you walk in obedience and in the directions given by the Word of God there is no room for rebellion. You are thankful because goodness and mercy has begun to follow you throughout the day. As you read on throughout the various gates your determination will grow to follow Jesus and you will not allow anything to stop you. Your conclusion will be to see Jesus in peace and in the safety of His love. Jesus knows the way that you take in right living and holy devotionals unto Him because you do not want to perish with the ungodly; **Psalms 1:6** – For the Lord knows the way of the righteous: but the way of the ungodly shall perish. Walking in the Sheep Gate, you recognize it is not about you but it is all about Jesus. Jesus is the chief corner stone and must not be rejected. One day, Jesus, the Chief Shepherd will appear, **I Peter 5:4** and He will give you a crown of life on that day. Your appetite is beginning to be filled up with love for yourself and others. You want to tell everyone about Jesus and what He has done in your life. How He saved you from the world of sin and invited you to follow Him. Your whole life has been turned around to do well on your job, treat your neighbor right and love your enemies. Show forth the love as you witness to other and you will catch the fish because the Lord has made you fishers of men, **Matthew 4:19** – And he saith unto them, Follow me, and I will make you fishers of men. Let your life speak for you. Stay in the Sheep Gate and possess the newness of life that only the Lord has given you and the devil can't take away. As you progress through this gate, you are now dead to sin, **Romans 8:10** – And if Christ be in you, the body is dead because of sin; but the Spirit is life because of righteousness. You now belong to God the Father, God the Son and God the Holy Ghost. Right now, you are now the righteousness of God and you will have great success in the Fish Gate. You have a right to be an ambassador of the Lord to your friends and enemies. In the Sheep's Gate with each passing day, you will love Jesus more today than yesterday. Daily you must walk with the Lord, read the Word of God and listen to the guidance of the Spirit of God. The Lord will become sweeter and sweeter with each passing day, **Psalm 119:103** – How sweet are thy words unto my taste. You will begin to taste and see that the Lord is good. Stay in the Sheep Gate, mature and grow according to the Word of God and you will become fishers of men. This unsaved society needs to know of the "Hope" that lives in you because the experience in the Sheep Gate. Now it is time to be a witness for your Lord. Tell the Lord, you will be a witness for Him in the Fish Gate.

2

Fish Gate – Nehemiah 3:3

From the Sheep Gate to the Fish Gate, your walk with the Lord has just begun. This walk becomes more and more precious to you with every waking hour. You want the whole world to know who Jesus is and what He is to you personally but most of all spiritually. Now, the Lord has called you to become fishers of men, **Matthew 4:19** – And he saith unto them, Follow me, and I will make you fishers of men. No one else can do what God has called for you to do in the Fish Gate. You may not be a preacher but the whole world has become your stage to witness so that the Lord will get the glory out of your life. The world may have the magnifying glass to find fault but you know the Magnifier and His Name is Jesus. Let the Magnifier illuminate out of your life love for lost men, women, boys and girls. Your witness is that you want everyone to know and love the Lord. You want to share your testimony and your love for God and mankind. The Lord has captured you by His love and now you are commissioned to capture others for the Lord by His love. You will see that you have work to do in Christ Jesus by the guidance of the Fish Gate. This gate is a very busy gate because it takes action on your part to do the fishing for mankind's souls. Sometimes that action is positive and sometimes the action can become negative. Remember where there is a positive, negative is somewhere around. You must work through the negative by the process of love. This love must first be in your heart to flow to the heart of the one you are witnessing to. As you look at the unsaved souls today, you must remember where God brought you from and where the Lord is leading you to by His grace, **I Corinthians 15:10** – But by the grace of God I am what I am: and his grace which was bestowed upon me was not in vain; but I labored more abundantly that they all: yet not I, but the grace of God which was with me. Your only desire is that you want everyone to know who Jesus is and like the Lord desires that no man is lost in eternity's realm. You have accepted the job of witnessing for the Lord. Few will accept this call of God because it is not glamorous. Many times it is when no one will see you witnessing but God Himself. God will see you kneeling and praying over the lost souls of this world. The harvest is ripe but the laborers are few, **Matthew 9:37-38** – Then saith he unto his disciples, the harvest truly is plenteous, but the laborers are few. Pray ye therefore the Lord of the harvest, that he will send forth laborers into his harvest. Like the 12 disciples that Jesus called, their lives begun when they accepted the call of Jesus from their occupations. Your acceptance came in the Fish Gate when you accepted the call to let your life shine before men showing a difference between good and evil and they began to see good works out of your life and that God has done something in your life, **Matthew 5:16** –Let your light so shine before men, that they may see your good works, and glorify your Father which is in heaven. Rather on your natural job, grocery store, in the gym, the Lord must be seen by everyone who does not know the Lord. The Lord has given you a light which no man or circumstance of life should put out or diminish. You will have an adversity of people to talk to and help them to know who Jesus is. You must first get familiar with their religion, rather Muslim, Baptist, Pentecostal, Catholic or Atheist. Yes, Atheist. They believe in something. They believe that there is no God. When a fisherman goes fishing, he catches a variety of fish, **Ezekiel 47:10** - ....they shall be a place to spread forth nets; their fish shall be according to their kinds, as the fish of the great sea, exceeding many. These will be all of mankind, black, white, short, tall, rich and poor. All with red blood that flows to show according to the Word of God, there is life in the blood, **Leviticus 17:11** – For the life of the flesh is in the blood: and I have given it to you upon the altar to make an atonement for your souls: for it is the blood that make an atonement for the soul. First beyond a shadow of a doubt, you must know first that Jesus loves you and He shredded His blood for the atonement of your soul. And then you can tell others that Jesus loves them too. You must have faith and believe that you are saved because of the Blood of Jesus. Love is the first fact that must be demonstrated and shown and the other fruits will come forth as you witness and continue in the love that Jesus displayed to you, **John 15:9** – As the Father hath loved me, so have I loved you: continue ye in my love. You will need to show fruits in your life that will display the change in your life and that you have been with Jesus, **Galatians 5:22-23** - But the fruit of the Spirit is love, joy, peace, longsuffering, gentleness, goodness, faith, meekness, temperance: against such there is no law. Make sure your fruits are fit for witnessing on any given day. No rotten fruits are acceptable in witnessing for the Lord. When Jesus met the woman by the well, He knew all about her. There will be some that you witness to and you may know something about them; however, witness with the Fruits of the Spirit without condemnation. Those you witness to with the fruits of the Spirit will like the woman by the well because they have had an encounter with Jesus through your witnessing to them, **John 4:29** – Come, see a man, which told me all things that ever I did: is not this the Christ? They will recognize Jesus and Jesus only. Jesus was the first fisher of men when He called His disciples, **Mark 1:16**. This is why Jesus is the only One Who can make you fishers of men but first you must be sanctified in your heart, **I Peter 3:15** – But sanctify the Lord God in your hearts: and be ready always to give an answer to every man that ask you a reason of the hope that is in you with meekness and fear. You have to be able to witness in meekness and fear because people are watching your life style. Are you displaying a sanctified life in action by what comes out of your mouth? It is the sanctification of the inner man and not the outward appearance. You have told the Lord that you will go and witness and be a walking testimony in the Fish Gate. As you follow the Lord, the Good Shepherd is watching your progress and then in your spirit you will want to become fishers of men and be the one that is called out to be a witness for the Lord. Jesus called 12 disciples to learn and only one did not learn, Judas. Don't betray Jesus by going against the Lord's guidance. You have reached your confidence in the Shepherd of your soul and want to tell someone what the Lord has done in your life. You want people to taste, like you have tasted and see what the Lord has done for you and you will tell others to come, **Psalm 34:8** – O taste and see that the Lord is good: blessed is the man that trusts in him. It is rewarding to witness because it will bring other sheep into the pasture to be kept by the Lord. In the Fish Gate, you must be instructed by the Lord how, when, and where to go and witness. Remember the disciples fished all night long and caught no fish until Jesus told them what to do, **John 21:6**. You must never let your testimony be pushy but seasoned with the love of God. You must know that God has sent you and be confident in the fact that the devil will be defeated in someone's life on that day, **Luke 4:19** – To preach the acceptable year of the Lord. You will begin to recognize the condition of others around you rather on your job, family, the church and the lost world in general. You have accepted this great commission from the Lord, **Mark 16:15** – And he said unto them, Go ye into all the world, and preach the gospel to every creature. The best words are displayed by action and in deeds. Let the life that you live speak for you. Many will and probably have never picked up a Bible; however, you can and must be the best walking Bible for mankind to read. You become the best walking billboard spokesperson Word of God. You must tell someone about the love of Jesus and your experience since accepting the Lord into your life, just lift Jesus, **John 12:32** – And I, if I be lifted up from the earth, will draw all men unto me. Jesus is the drawer of men unto Himself. You are not ashamed, **Romans 1:16** – For I am not ashamed of the gospel of Christ: for it is the power of God unto salvation to everyone that believeth: to the Jew first, and also to the Greek. Your church's mission/evangelical classes are the training field for witnessing but as you learn the Word of God the outside of the four walls of the church becomes your mission field. As you stand out in the open air, a street corner, your life for Christ to be displayed, that soul is waiting for you to come and introduce them to your Lord and Savior. Remember, you can change the world, "one man, and one soul, at a time." You will have the desire to witness in the White House to the drug houses, every street corner and highway and witness for the Lord as the love of God grows in your heart for others to know the Lord, **James 5:19-20** – Brethren, if any of you do err from the truth, and one convert him; Let him know, that he which convert the sinner from the error of his way shall save a soul from death, and shall hide a multitude of sins. You will just want to give the Lord thanks as the feeling of gratitude sweeps over your sanctified soul. Also a sad note in the Fish Gate, not everyone will adhere to the Word of God some will be just almost persuaded, **Acts 26:28** – Then Agrippa said unto Paul, Almost thou persuadest me to be a Christian. Many will not accept your testimony or your witness but you just may be one that just plants the Word of God and then the Lord will send another to come along and water, but it is God that gives the increase because we are laborers together with God, **I Corinthians 3:6-9**. You must not get discouraged but continue to witness for the Lord, **Luke 9:5** – And whosoever will not receive you, when ye go out of that city, shake off the very dust from your feet for a testimony against them. You are just a messenger sent from God and many will try to shoot the messenger. You can slap the devil in the face by witnessing what the Lord has done for you and remember where the Lord has brought you from, **I Timothy 1:15** – This is a faithful saying, and worthy of all acceptation, that Christ Jesus came into the world to save sinners, of whom I am chief. Never witness with a sinless testimony. Remember all have sinned and come short of the glory of God. Witness about what the Lord has delivered you from and you will win a soul for the Lord and this makes you wise. It is sad to watch an unsaved man or woman and now even a child that is at the age of accountability would reject the love of God. You must always remember they are not rejecting you but they are rejecting God, **I Thessalonians 5:8** – He therefore that despise, despise not man, but God, who hath also given unto us his Holy Spirit. Mankind is rebelling against the Word of God. However, keep witnessing because you are wise in the eyesight of God, **Proverbs 11:30** – The fruit of the righteous is a tree of life; and he that wins souls is wise. As you witness you will see how far mankind has departed from God. You must be steadfast and unmovable, always abounding in the Word of God and know that your labor is not in vain, **I Corinthians 15:58**. Your compassion for witnessing is seen from your heart that comes out throughout your eyes, **Matthew 6:22** – The light of the body is the eye, if therefore thine eye be single; thy whole body shall be full of light. As you speak to a person, heart to heart, you will begin to know and understand how they feel and they will hear the compassion in our voice and see the love in your eyes. Your countenance will tell the story of what occurred in your life how the Lord took you out of darkness and into His marvelous light, **I Peter 2:9.** Your appearance must show the "holiness" of God and you long for others to experience what the Lord can do in their lives on a daily basis. Witnessing is not only in word but in the way the world looks at you. You must let your light so shine that men will see your good works and glorify your Father who is in heaven, **Matthew 5:16**. The eyes of people are upon you and in fact their eyes become magnifying glasses that will watch your every move. You must be different in conversation, manner of life, walk and attitude toward everyone you meet. Even if that person is a stranger, be careful how you interact with him or her, you may be entertaining an angel of the Lord that was sent to encourage you as you encourage them, **Hebrews 13:2** - Be not forgetful to entertain strangers: for thereby some have entertained angels unawares. You greet your brother or your sister in Christ with a holy kiss but the unsaved you will greet with joy and love to draw them toward God, **Jeremiah 31:3** – The Lord hath appeared of old unto me, saying, Yea, I have loved thee with an everlasting love: therefore with loving-kindness have I drawn thee. Show forth the attributes of the Christian life you are living representing and serving the True and Living God. Find yourself a fellow fisherman because the Lord sent them out by twos, **Luke 10:1-23** – …the harvest is great but the laborers are few…lambs among wolves. Take no scrip…proclaim peace wherever you enter…heal the sick…speak of Jesus…and blessed are the eyes which see the thing that ye see. Witnessing is work and this is why the Lord said, He will pay you, **Hebrew 6:10** – For God is not unrighteous to forget your work and labour of love, which ye have shewed toward his name and on that day He will say, "Well done, good and faithful servant, **Matthew 25:21** – His lord said unto him, well done, thou good and faithful servants: thou hast been faithful over a few things, I will make thee ruler over many things: enter thou into the joy of thy Lord. Always remember, witnessing for the Lord is a work of faith. You must keep your labor with much love attached. Most of all, you must have patience with hope always in Christ Jesus. Just witness and work, while it is day, for when night comes, no man can work, **John 9:4**. Witnessing for the Lord helps to sharpen your tools in the Word of God. The Sword of the Spirit is the Word of God and it is sharpened to destroy satan's devices offensively and defensively. Look yourself in the mirror and dress for the occasion according to **Ephesians 6:10-18** – Finally, be strong...put on the whole arm of God...prepared to stand...to stand in the evil day...with truth....in righteousness...taking faith...dressed with the gospel of peace...having the mind of salvation...the word of God...and praying always. Witnessing helps you to establish the Word of God in your heart and you will settle in at the Old Gate with no problems and no variations. You have begun to live the life, working the plan that has been laid out for you in God's process for you and it is beginning to look really good, **Jeremiah 29:11** – For I know the thoughts that I think toward you, saith the Lord, thoughts of peace, and not of evil, to give you an expected end. Keep processing for that expected end is for your good, **Romans 8:28** – And we know that all things work together for good to them that love God, to them who are the called according to his purpose. Others will believe your report and agree with the words that proceed out of your mouth, **Isaiah 53:1** – Who hath believed our report:? And to whom is the arm of the Lord revealed? The arm of the Lord is a mighty arm that those that will believe will lean upon and believe because of your report that you believe. Walking out of the Fish Gate, you have just become God's gift to the world because of the ability to reach the lost at any cost. How are you developing in the Word of God? Have you hid the Word of God in our heart, **Psalm 119:11** – Thy word have I hid in mine heart, that I might not sin against thee, that you will not sin against the Lord? The Old Gate shows you the pathway to follow, "the Way", to obtain the Truth and obtain the life in Jesus Christ, **John 14:6** – Jesus saith unto him, I am the way, the truth, and the life: no man cometh unto the Father, but by me. Welcome to the Old Gate that will teach you the ways of "Holiness".

3

The Old Gate – Nehemiah 3:6

From the Sheep Gate to the Fish Gate, you are beginning to understand the ways of the Lord because of His word. The Word of God without alternative routes is your road map to follow on the path of holiness in the Lord. You have begun to study your Bible, **II Timothy 2:15** – Study to shew thyself approved unto God, a workman that needed not to be ashamed, rightly dividing the word of truth. Your mind has begun to grasp the true teachings to follow the Word of God from the Old Testament to the New Testament. The Word of God has become a living epistle in your mind, body and soul and has enlightened your path, **Psalm 119:105** – Thy word is a lamp unto my feet, and a light unto my path. The Lord will honor your request when you seek Him in the Old Gate, **Psalm 27:11** – Teach me thy way, O Lord, and lead me in a plain path, because of mine enemies. You will encounter enemies of your soul that will say that it does not take all that and you don't need to read your Bible or even pray. The Lord will hide you from the enemy of your soul, satan, because you are in the Old Gate. This gate wants to develop in you righteousness, peace and joy in the Holy Ghost. The closing stages, when you walk out of the Old Gate, there is no other god but the True and Living God and He is faithful and true, **Revelation 19:11** – And I saw heaven opened, and behold a white horse; and he that sat upon him was called Faithful and True, and in righteousness he doth judge and make war. His Name is Jesus, the Son of the Living God. The Bible has begun to be developed in our heart, mind and soul. You know that there is no other Savior but Jesus, **Isaiah 43:11** – I, even I, am the Lord; and beside me there is no savior. Your heart is fixed to trust in the Lord, no matter what comes and what goes, because of His Word that tells you never be afraid to walk in the Old Path, **Psalm 112:7** – He shall not be afraid of evil tidings; his heart is fixed, trusting in the Lord. Your mind, according to the Word of God is determined and made up to follow after Jesus' ways and your mind is sold out to follow Him. In the Old Gate, you know who your soul belongs to and the Old Gate shows you that one day, that soul will return back to the One who breathed into it and your soul became a living soul, **Genesis 2:7**. You have found the Lord to be your shepherd and He has allowed you to become a true witness unto Himself. The old man has passed away and the new man has been developed in you and can't do things your way because your way is not God's way and your thoughts are not God's thoughts, **Isaiah 55:8-9** – For my thoughts are not your thoughts, neither are your ways my ways, saith the Lord. For as the heavens are higher than the earth, so are my ways higher than your ways, and my thoughts than your thoughts. You must have and keep the mind of Christ in the Old Gate, Let this mind be in you which was in Christ Jesus, **Philippines 2:5**. The disciples sat in the presence of the Lord to be taught from the Master's plan for their lives. Jesus knew them from the learners to the betrayer. The Master's plan is set up in the Word of God for God's people and we cannot convert from the Word of God. It does not matter how smooth it may look, it just might look crooked in the eyesight of God. You must continue to walk in the strait and narrow way that Jesus walked with His disciples. They began to listen intensely to the Word that proceeded out of the mouth of the Lord to the point they wanted to know how to pray, **Luke 11:1** – And it came to pass, that, as he was praying in a certain place, when he ceased, one of his disciples said unto him, Lord, teach us to pray, as John also taught his disciples. It took just one disciple; it only takes you to ask the Lord to teach you how to pray. It takes the Spirit of God within you to pray because we don't know what to pray for, **Romans 8:26-27** – Likewise the Spirit also helped our infirmities: for we know not what we should pray for as we ought: but the Spirit itself make intercession for us with groaning which cannot be uttered. And he that searches the hearts know what is the mind of the Spirit, because he makes intercession for the saints according to the will of God. It is not old fashion to pray because men should always pray and not faint, **I Thessalonians 5:16**. In the Old Gate as you pray, you will develop the attributes of God. You will grow in the characteristics of God's holiness, **Psalm 99:9** – Exalt the Lord our God, and worship at his holy hill; for the Lord our God is holy and you will develop into the features of God's righteousness and will not divert from the ways of the Word of God, **I John 1:9** – Whosoever is born of God doth not commit sin; for his seed remaineth in him: and he cannot sin, because he is born of God. You will begin to talk to the Lord privately and openly for a closer encounter with the Lord. You see Jesus only, **Matthew 17** - And when they had lifted up their eyes, they saw no man, saved Jesus only. The Old Gate is the combination of the Old and New Testament in action in a believer's life. No you don't ride around on camels, eat certain foods, or go on top of a mountain and build altars to worship God. However, the God of the Old Testament has not changed. You still have to draw close to the Lord with a pure heart and be blessed, **Matthew 5:8**. You cannot have a drawback spirit. Listen to every word that the preacher is speaking to you concerning the old path that is straight and narrow. You see the God of the Old Testament and the Lord Jesus of the New Testament are the same and you must accept the Word of God at "Faith" value. Times and things may change but don't you change with times or things when it comes to the Word of God. God does not change and He does not want his people to change, **Malachi 3:6** and He expects us to walk accordingly in the old path He created for us to walk, **Jeremiah 6:16** – Thou saith the Lord, Stand ye in the ways, and see, and ask for the old paths, where is the good way, and walk therein, and ye shall find rest for your souls But they said, We will not walk therein. If you don't understand, ask the Lord and He will show you the old path. The old path represents obedience to the Word of God and not rebellion. Yes, the Lord said that He would do a "New Thing". The new thing in these last days is the anointing of the Holy Ghost for a closer walk with the Lord to bring prosperity into the lives of His people, **Isaiah 43:18-19** – Behold, I will do a new thing; now it shall spring forth; shall ye not know it? I will even make a way in the wilderness, and rivers in the desert. God's new thing will bring newness of life to His people. This is why the

Lord tells us not to remember the former things; neither considers the things of old because the Lord desires to do new things in our lives. You cannot be like the world and become worldly under the leadership of the Good Shepherd. Jesus will tell you to come out from among them and be separate, **II Corinthians 6:12** – Wherefore come out from among them (the world/unbelievers), and be ye separate (do not partake of sin), saith the Lord, and touch not the unclean thing (unrighteous things which cause sin to settle in your spirit), and I will receive you (Jesus' leading and guidance). When you reject God's Word and the elements of His Word, you reject God. Be not like the children of Israel, they wanted a king because the world around them had kings. Just as Jesus taught the people on the hill side, Jesus has taught you His way that was not your ways and has given you His thoughts that are not your thoughts, **Isaiah 55:8-9** – For my thoughts are not your thoughts, neither are your ways my ways, saith the Lord. For as the heavens are higher than the earth, so are my ways higher than your ways, and my thoughts than your thoughts. God is not coming down to your level but in the old path, you must reach up to the Lord's level and when you think you have reached it, the Lord will move up a little higher for you to reach higher too. This is the way you will be able to abide in the Old Gate is to have the mind of Christ, **Philippians 2:5**. The world will call you old fashion because you don't fit the world's mold, however, you must remember, the world does not know the ways of your God. You have made the difference between clean and unclean and holy and unholy, **Leviticus 10:10** – And that ye may put difference between holy and unholy, and between unclean and clean. The difference between darkness and light and evil and

good, you no longer call good evil and evil good, **Isaiah 5:20** –
Woe unto them that call evil good, and good evil; that put
darkness for light, and light for darkness; that put bitter for sweet,
and sweet for bitter! The Old Gate is where you stand confident
in Christ Jesus because of the standards of the Bible annotated in
the Old and New Testament. You have matured in the doctrines
of the Lord Jesus Christ. You have tasted, ate and have begun to
digest the sixty-six of the Word of God, **Ezekiel 3:1-3**, and have
accepted the Word of God as your guide. Many think that the
Old Testament does not apply to the church today, but it does,
things that were written beforehand were written for our learning,
Romans 15:4. Yes, the Lord is a God of love but also God is a
God of wrath. The Old Gate may become old fashioned because
of peer pressure. This pressure can be in the pulpit and in the
congregation. The Old Gate will never be "old fashioned" and
should be never broken down in your life. The standards of the
Word of God will never change from the Old Testament to the
New Testament because they are settled in heaven, **Psalm 119:89**.
In the Old Gate you have accepted the Word of God that you will
not sin against God, **Psalm 119:11**. You remember the Sheep
Gate and how you began to walk with the Lord and the Lord
began to teach you His Word and the "Holy" standards have been
established in your mind, body and soul. The Old Gate keeps you
in love with God following the path of "salvation." You have
accepted that straight is the gate and narrow is the way and a few
shall find and this is the old path, **Matthew 7:13-14** – Enter ye
in at the strait gate: for wide is the gate, and broad is the way, that
leadeth to destruction, and many there be which go in thereat:
Because strait is the gate, and narrow is the way, which leadeth

unto lie, and few there be that find it. However, you have found the old path. Many are leaving the old path and have found a new way that will lead many to destruction. You have accepted the Word of God at "Faith" value. You have heard the Word of God from your grandma's lab, from the voice of the preachers, and from your personal study time and has come to the conclusion that God's Word will not return to Him void but it will accomplish whatever you need as long as you stay in the Old Path, **Isaiah 55:11** – So shall my word be that goeth forth out of my mouth: it shall not return unto me void, but it shall accomplish that which I please, and it shall prosper in the thing whereto I sent it. Many feel today that they have found a better way outside the Word of God. You began to see the difference between clean and unclean, holy and unholy, **Ezekiel 44:23**. These standards are so much in your spiritual being and in your love for God; you do not touch the unclean things of the world or do the unclean things of world, **I John 2:15** – Love not the world, neither the things that are in the world. If any man love the world, the love of the Father is not in him. Do not love the things of this world. This brings on the lust of the flesh, the lust of the eyes and the of pride life. This is not of God but of the world. You come to realize that God of the Old Gate does not change, **Psalm 102:27** – But thou art the same, and thy years shall have no end, and neither does His Holy Word, the Bible. In the Old Gate, no devil in hell can come and take you off the sure foundation, Jesus Christ because the light of God in your life will expose the suggestions of darkness, **Ephesians 5:11** – And have no fellowship with the unfruitful works of darkness, but rather reprove them. The best part of the Old Gate is the discipline in the Word of God that will be established in your walk with God. You will walk in the doctrine in the Old Testament into the New Testament that leads you to righteousness in Christ Jesus that is pleasing to God. The worse part of the Old Gate is when you fail yourself because you have found a better way outside the Word of God. There is no better way. The better way is the board way which leads to destruction, **Matthew 7:13-14** – Enter ye in at the strait gate: for wide is the gate, and board is the way, that leadth to destruction, and many there be which go in thereat: Because strait is the gate, and narrow is the way, which leadeth into life, and few there be that find it. The goats walk in the better way and keep hitting their heads. The tares grow in the better way and are good for nothing. The sheep will stay in the straight and narrow path that leads to life eternal. When you think you have found a better way outside the Word of God, you become one of the children of disobedience with the characteristics of disobedience, **Ephesians 5:3-7** – For this ye know, that no whoremonger, nor unclean person, nor covetous man, who is an idolater, hath any inheritance in the kingdom of Christ and of God. Let no man deceive you with vain words: for because of these things cometh the wrath of God upon the children of disobedience. Be not ye therefore partakers with them. You must always remember God's Word does not change and is everlasting to everlasting, **Isaiah 40:8** – The grass withereth, the flower fadeth: but the word of our God shall stand for ever. You do not want to be found weighing in the balance, **Daniel 5:27**. The Word of God will give your life balance. The Word of God helps you to know right from wrong, true from false and light from darkness. Remember, the Word of God is right; somebody is wrong. Let God be truth and every man a liar,

Psalm 116:11 – I said in my haste, all men are liars. Never fall into the category of adding or subtracting from the Word of God. If you take away from the Word of God, you may found yourself being guilty of it all, **James 2:10**, and the plagues in the Word of God will be your demise, **Deuteronomy 4:2** – Ye shall not add unto the word which I command you, neither shall ye diminish ought from it, that ye may keep the commandments of the Lord your God which I command you and **Revelation 22:19** – And if any man shall take away from the words of the book of this prophecy, God shall take away his part out of the book of life, and out of the holy city, and from the things which are written in this book. God spoke in the Old Testament and Jesus spoke in the New Testament and we must live the Word according to both Testaments. The world want to change the Word of God to show weakness in the Bible; however, we serve the everlasting Father God, the Holy God and His strength says what it means and means what it says. The Word of God is eternal, **Psalm 119:89** – For ever, O Lord, thy word is settled in heaven and God does not change. Never lose your appetite for the ways of "Holiness" and never let the Word of God sour in your life, for without "Holiness", no man will see the Lord, **Hebrews 12:14**, "Stay". Remember your teachings in the Old Gate help you survive in all of the remaining gates because man shall not live by bread alone but by every word that proceeds out of the mouth of God, **Matthew 4:4**. The Old Gate is the path of holiness, righteousness that gives you the love, mercy, and the grace of God in your life. So, you must just travel down this straight and narrow way, **Matthew 7:13-14** – Enter ye in at the strait gate: for wide is the gate, and broad is the way that leadeth to destruction, and many there be which go in thereat: Because strait is the gate, and narrow is the way; which leadeth unto life and few there be that find it. Don't let any devil in hell sway your heart or mind into another direction that is contrary to the Word of God. Never be blindsided by satan or false teachings concerning the Word of God. Strength is gained as you go through the Old Gate and when you reach the Valley Gate the strength of the Word of God will be manifested because of your development in the Word of God in the Old Gate. It is time now to enter the Valley Gate with the Word of God in your heart. Trials may cause suffering but remember God is too holy to do harm and too righteous to do wrong while you enter into the Valley Gate.

4

The Valley Gate – Nehemiah 3:13

Remember always, you are in this world but you are not of this world and Jesus has prayed for you to be kept while you are in this present world, **John 17:15-16**, The Valley Gate presents circumstances of life, i.e., trials, tribulations, sickness, poverty, etc. In the Valley Gate always remember we are in this world and you will go through with the world conditions but we have the confidence and guarantee that Jesus will bring us out without a doubt. Faith will take you through and keep in mind, trouble does not last always. In the Valley Gate, the mature saint of God is separated from the regular church goer. The Valley Gate is just a test of your faith. Sometimes your faith may get small but keep the mustard seed faith, **Matthew 17:20** – And Jesus said unto them, because of your unbelief: for verily I say unto you, if ye have faith as a grain of mustard seed, ye shall say unto this mountain, remove hence to yonder place; and it shall remove; and nothing shall be impossible unto you. Confidence will draw you closer and closer to the Lord and you will see what God can do in any valley of your life because He is a God of the valley, **I**

Kings 20:28 – And there came a man of God, and spake unto the king of Israel, and said, thus saith the Lord, Because the Syrians have said, the Lord is God of the hills, but he is not God of the valleys, therefore will I deliver all this great multitude into thine hand, and ye shall know that I am the Lord. Hold fast to your faith in what God can and will do. God is a deliver no matter the valley, i.e., depression, sickness, guilt, sorrow; He will deliver you from your enemies in the valley of your life's circumstances. Yes, the Valley Gate is uncomfortable and not a pleasant place to reside. Keep in mind at all times, the Valley Gate is not your resting place and this also will pass over in God's time frame because He is a God of the valley. There will be areas in your life that will be uncomfortable places, however, there must be no fear, **II Timothy 1:7** – For God has not given us the spirit of fear; but of power, and of love, and of a sound mind. Satan causes fear, not the Lord. Fear is torment, **I John 4:18** and satan come to torment in your thought patterns, health, and relationships. You must always speak life into a situation because there is power in the tongue, **Proverbs 18:21**. Life and death will always be around us. They are holding hands and walking with us daily. Claim life into yourself on a daily basis by speaking the Word of God, **Psalm 23:4** – Yea, though I walk through the valley of the shadow of death, I will fear no evil: for thou art with me; thy rod and thy staff they comfort me. The Valley Gate is where you experience trials and tribulations in the life your life because you are one of the precious sheep in the Lord's pasture. In the Valley Gate, there is no fear because the Lord is in the Valley Gate with you, **Hebrews 13:5** – Let your conversation be without covetousness, and be content with such things as ye have: for he hath said, I will never leave thee, nor forsake thee. You will always be guided and lead by the Lord, **Exodus 13:21** – And the Lord went before them by day in a pillar of a cloud, to lead them the way; and by night in a pillar of fire, to give them light: to go by day and night: He took not away the pillar of the cloud by day, nor the pillar of fire by night, from before the people. Just as the Lord was with the children of Israel, He is with you today. You find strength in the Valley Gate because your confidence is in Jesus and not yourself, and you have come to the conclusion that He will put no more on you than you can bear, **I Corinthians 10:13** – There hath no temptation taken you but such as is common to man: but God is faithful, who will not suffer you to be tempted above that ye are able; but will with the temptation also make a way to escape, that ye may be able to bear it. The Valley Gate is a valley of life's circumstances, i.e., death, physical and emotional illnesses, financial hardships, divorce, to name a few that invades human lives, Christian or non-Christian. You will be maintained only by the Word of God, **Psalm 121:7** – The Lord shall preserve thee from all evil: he shall preserve thy soul. In the Valley Gate, you must stay in the Word of God by reading and mediating upon the promises of God. Always remember, God honors His Word. The Lord will send His word and heal you and the Word will not return unto Him void. Keep your faith in Him, **Psalm 107:20** – He sent his word and healed them, and delivered them from their destructions and **Isaiah 55:11** – So shall my word be that goeth forth out of my mouth: it shall not return unto me void, but it shall accomplish that which I please, and it shall prosper in the thing whereto I sent it. You will praise God in any valley circumstance due to His wondrous works toward your circumstances in the Valley Gate. Because of what you have learned in the Sheep Gate, Fish -Gate, Old Gate; there is no reason you will not survive in the Valley Gate. You are covered by the love of God and you must never forget you are in His powerful and capable hands in a secret place, **Psalm 91:1-2** – He that dwelleth in the secret place of the most High shall abide under the shadow of the Almighty. I will say of the Lord, He is my refuge, and my fortress: my God; in him will I trust. The Word of God did not say secret places. There is only one secret place in the Valley Gate and that secret place in the will of God. During the times of sorrow, destruction of property and failure of finances, you must find that place in the Word of God that you can abide until the storms of life have passed over. Suffering brings forth steadfast obedience in your life, **Hebrews 5:8** – Though he were a Son, yet learned he obedience by the things which he suffered. Jesus suffered and you must arm yourself likewise. Man is of a few day but full of trouble, **Job 4:1**, however, God can deliver you from all of your troubles, when you call on the Name of the Lord, **Psalm 50:15** – And call upon me in the day of trouble: I will deliver thee, and thou shalt glory me. Throughout your life, you will have painful experiences. There are no escaping life's ups and downs. Circumstances of life can put you in the Valley Gate, however, always remember, the Lord loves you with mercy, and compassion that will not fail you, **Lamentations 3:22-23** – It is of the Lord's mercies that we are not consumed, because his compassions fail not. The Valley Gate shows you the love, mercy and compassion of the Lord. The Lord is too holy to do wrong and too righteous to do harm. Never become the prisoner of suffering but remain the prisoner of Jesus Christ.

When Paul and Silas were in jail they did not become the prisoner of their circumstance but they sang songs, remembering the goodness of the Lord, **Acts 16:23-25** – And when they had laid many stripes upon them, they cast them into prison, charging the jailer to keep them safely. And at midnight Paul and Silas prayed, and sang praises unto God: and the prisoners heard them. Others are watching you in the Valley Gate, especially the world will be watching. They are watching your reaction. They will ask where your God is, **Psalm 42:10** - …my enemies reproached me; while they say daily unto me, Where is thy God? Will you still believe God? Count your blessings and name them one by one and know that God can do whatever to bring you out of any circumstance that has risen. You must count your blessings and not the days in the Valley Gate. Think on the "goodness of Jesus" and all they He has done for you, count the blessings and even name them and put the blessings in the face of the enemy and faint not, **Psalm 27:13-14** – I had fainted unless I had believed to see the goodness of the Lord in the land of the living. You must wait on the Lord and believe that He will deliver you. The Lord is an on time God. In all circumstances in your life, Jesus is the present help in the time of trouble. Jesus is God. Also, remember, to take one day at a time, **Psalm 118:24** – This is the day that the Lord has made; we will rejoice and be glad in it. The Valley Gate helps you to experience going through whatever life situations presents and truly learn how "good" God is and how real the love of God is pointed toward your life. Never forget to pray as you stay in the Valley Gate. Talk to the Lord, He is your friend and most of the time in the Valley Gate the Lord is the only One to talk too sometimes. This day and age, many people cannot know how you feel because many are going through their own Valley Gate. Jesus is your only friend that sticks closer than a brother, **Proverbs 18:24**. You will have a testimony to give to others that will help them to know they can process though the Valley Gate and give the devil's face a big slap showing your growth in the Lord. You did not give up or give in and this will enable you to help others not to faint. Keep yourself in the best sense of humor possible, **Proverbs 17:22**. Keep your feelings in check and in perspective as you evaluate the situation. Evaluate the day, rest in the Lord and read your Bible as the day ends and don't forget to pray, close your eyes and take your rest, **Hebrews 4:9** – There remaineth therefore a rest to the people of God. Remind yourself how blessed you are no matter the outcome of the circumstance that has brought you into the Valley Gate. It may have been a death of a loved one, change in relationships, or just your short comings concerning your walk with the Lord. Walk by faith and not by sight, **II Corinthians 5:7**. Always remember, the Lord is always there with you in the Valley Gate. The Valley Gate is a lonely place but the Good Shepherd, Jesus, will never leave you are forsake you, **Hebrew 15:12**. Remember, His eyes are on the sparrow and just know that Jesus watches over you, **Matthew 10:29-30** – Are not two sparrows sold for a farthing? And one of them shall not fall on the ground without your Father. But the very hairs of your head are all numbered. Fear ye not therefore, ye are of more value than many sparrows. The Lord is the keeper of the Valley Gate and the Lord is faithful, **I Corinthians 1:9** – God is faithful, by whom ye were called unto the fellowship of his Son Jesus Christ, our Lord. There is nothing that you go through in the Valley Gate that He has not made a way of escape for you and the Lord knows how to deliver you, **Psalm 34:17** – The righteous cry, and the Lord heareth, and delivereth them out of all their troubles. Your way of escape will always be according to the Word of God. Satan will always try to make you abort what you need to learn in the Valley Gate. You need to learn that God is a deliver and a healer. From the first day to the last day, keep a journal that is read by only you. Write, rather a good day, how you felt during the day, did you experience a lack of faith, what made you happy or sad and was it a good day or a bad day. You will see your advance and you will see what is not allowing you to believe God. Rather in the valley of temptation or illness, you have a way of escape that is given only by the Lord, **I Corinthians 10:13**. The best part of the Valley Gate you truly learn that the Lord is the Chief Shepherd. You will receive all the benefits, blessed, forgiven, redeemed and good things from the Lord, because of the experience, **Psalm 103:2-5** – Bless the Lord, O my soul: and forget not all his benefits; who forgiveth all thine iniquities; who healeth all thy diseases; who redeemeth thy life from destruction; who crowneth thee with lovingkindness and tender mercies; who satisfieth thy mouth with good things; so that thou youth is renewed like the eagles. In the Valley Gate you can be renewed and restored; naturally and spiritually. The Lord will take care of your problems, questions, and concerns of life especially when you pray. Sometimes in the Valley Gate, there's nothing else to do but "Pray". The worse part of the Valley Gate is when you take problems, questions and the concerns of life into our own hands and try to fix it yourself. You will need just a little more grace to pull yourself up in the Word of God. You have to cast all your cares upon the Lord, **I Peter 5:7**, because He cares for you, **Psalm 55:22** – Cast thy burden upon the Lord, and he shall sustain thee: he shall never suffer the righteous to be moved. You must remain righteous and you will never be forsaken, **Psalm 37:25** – I have been young, and now am old; yet have I not seen the righteous forsaken, nor his seed begging bread. Rather you are young or old; you are covered by the Lord. In the Valley Gate, always remember the "Love of God", **Isaiah 41:10** – Fear thou not; for I am with thee: be not dismayed; for I am thy God: I will strengthen thee; yea, I will help thee; yea, I will uphold thee with the right hand of my righteous, fear not, God got you covered. The worse part of the Valley Gate is when you take things into your weak hands and think how to solve in your weak mind forgetting that you are grass, **Psalm 103:14**. The Lord already knows what you are made of and that is grass. In your weakest, allow the Spirit of the Holy Ghost help you wave to the Lord like the grass in the open field. Give the Lord a wave offering and praise His Name in the Valley Gate, **Psalm 150**. Always remember that trouble does not last always and the Lord will deliver you in His own timeframe. Remember it may be dark and cloudy today but the sun will come out tomorrow. Stay encouraged and stays strong, the sun may not be shining on you today, however, it is shining somewhere and you will have a sunny day again too. In the Valley Gate, don't be afraid or ashamed to cry because weeping may endure for the night but joy will come in the morning, **Psalm 30:5** and you will have your morning. Go through your midnight hour, the weakest hour. You must let the Lord take complete control during this hour. This midnight hour may be your weakest hour but it brings on another day. At your weakest hour, then the Lord, He is strong, **II Corinthians**

13:9 – For we are glad, when we are weak, and ye are strong: and this also we wish, even your perfection. In the Valley Gate, you are restored one day at a time. You must present satan a divergent; let him know that you will survive. Your tears are just a release and will be dried by your faith in God and what He is doing for you in the Valley Gate, **Romans 10:8** – For all things work together for the good to them that love God, to them who are the called according to his purpose. You must be fully persuaded and know that you have been called by God into this great salvation. You will never be the victim in the Valley Gate but you will be the victor. Remember the teaching of the Old Gate and you will never become like the dry bones in the valley, **Ezekiel 37:1-10** – The hand of the Lord was upon me and carried me out in the spirit of the Lord, and set me down in the midst of the valley which was full of bones. You have to take assessment of the situation in the Valley Gate. Situations of life love to hold the people of God hostage, a prisoner in the Valley Gate. Then the situation wants to manipulate you into unbelief and that God does not loves you while you are in the Valley Gate. This will cause you to become dry and brittle concerning the Word of God. And caused me to pass by them round about: and, behold, there were very many in the open valley; and lo, they were very dry. There were many in the open valley because you are not the only one that has passed this way before. The question is will you survive? Will you be the victor or will you become the victim and become like these dry bones while you are in the Valley Gate? Then the question was asked, And he said unto me, Son of man, can these bones live? And I answered, O Lord, thou knowest. The Lord is the only One Who knows when you will go into the Valley Gate and the Lord is the only One Who knows when you will come out of the Valley Gate. Just breathe and the Lord will breathe on you. Never let satan cut off your breath and never let him choke the life of God's Word out of your situation in the Valley Gate. Prophesy the Word of God to yourself. Keep your joy, peace and most of all keep your confidence in what the Lord can do. Do not throw your confidence away and keep the Word of God before your eyes in the Valley Gate, **Hebrews 10:35-36** – Cast not away therefore your confidence, which hath great recompense of reward. For ye have need of patience, that, after ye have done the will of God, ye might receive the promise. Now the just shall live by faith: but if any man draws back, my soul shall have no pleasure in him. But we are not of them who draw back unto perdition; but of them that believe to the saving of the soul. Be patient in the Valley Gate and draw closer and closer to the Lord by His Word, **Luke 21:9** – in your patience possess ye your souls. The question was asked; will you live or die in the Valley Gate? Will you give up on God in the Valley Gate? God knows. Again he said unto me, Prophesy upon these bones, and say unto them, O ye dry bones, hear the word of the Lord. Thus saith the Lord God unto these bones; behold, I will cause breath to enter into you, and ye shall live: And I will lay sinews upon you, and will bring up flesh upon you, and cover you with skin, and put breath in you, and you shall live; and ye shall know that I am the Lord. Be the amazing Christian, breakthrough every sealed up area, climb every mountain to reach the top, and break down every wall, even the walls of any Jericho. Don't you worry about tomorrow, let tomorrow take care of itself, **Matthew 6:34**. David had many valleys and mountains to cross from the pasture of sheep to the king's palace but he achieved the plan of God for his life. Just remember that the mercy and the compassion of the Lord are new every morning: great is His faithfulness toward you, **Lamentations 3:23**. Soon all the trials and tribulations will be over and we will rise up and walk into the place where the wicked shall cease from troubling and the weary shall be at rest and we all will cry halleluiah because there will be no more sickness and no more sorrow. Let the Valley Gate show you that joy will come in the morning when you see sorrow no more. Keep the Word of God near your heart with faith in God, In the Valley Gate; you may not be able to get to church. You might be on a bed of affliction or circumstances of life have slowed you down and you are unable to reach the door knob of the church and your encouragement must come from what you hear on the radio or TV ministry. Your preacher or elders of the church can't get to you in time so you must encourage yourself in the Lord by prophesying to yourself. Speak the Word of God to yourself. Just like King David encouraged himself in the Lord, **I Samuel 30:6** – And David was greatly distressed: but David encouraged himself in the Lord his God. Speak the Word of God out loud or in secret prayer with confidence in the God you serve, faith comes by hearing and hearing by the Word of God, **Romans 10:17**. The Lord will honor His Word when you speak with conviction concerning the Word of God. The Lord will cause something to happen and will move on your behalf. In the Valley Gate obedience is the key. You must do all that the Word of God has commanded you to do with no question and no compromise. No matter the time in this gate, God will send His Word and hasten to perform it, **Psalm 107:19-20** – Then they cry unto the Lord in their trouble, and he saveth them out of their distresses. He sent his word, and healed them, and delivered them from their destruction. Sometimes the cry will be silent but let it be the cry of faith from the heart to the Lord. There is life in the Word of God and it will be life to you in any situation. Stay refreshed, **Psalm 104:10** – He sendeth the springs into the valleys, which run among the hills. The Lord will give you times of refreshing in the Valley Gate, **Isaiah 41:18** – I will open rivers in high places and fountains in the midst of the valleys: I will make the wilderness a pool of water, and the dry land springs of water. Relax and know and depend on the God who cannot fail. There is nothing too hard for God, **Jeremiah 32:27** – Behold, I am the Lord, the God of all flesh: is there anything too hard for me? At the end of one of many Valley Gate visitations, each visit will make you stronger, stronger and stronger, **I Peter 5:10** – But the God of all grace, who hath called us unto his eternal glory by Christ Jesus, after that ye have suffered a while, make you perfect, stablish, strengthen, settle you. As you walk out of the Valley Gate, you will know that you are an overcomer by the Blood of the Lamb and have overcome by the great "I Am", Jesus. You are the victor and not the victim. Never become the victim of life's circumstances. Trouble does not last always and God will deliver you in His own timeframe. Your release will direct you to the Fountain for refreshing. Let's go and allow the Lord to lead you and drink from the fountain that never runs dry in the Fountain Gate and be refreshed by the Spirit of God.

5

The Fountain Gate – Nehemiah 3:16

Most likely in the Valley Gate you experienced times of dryness and experienced sandy areas in your spirit and now you must look for a place to refresh yourself in the Lord. The Spirit of God will lead you to the Fountain Gate. You must always remember that there is a rest for the people of God, **Hebrews 4:9** – There remaineth therefore a rest to the people of God. There is an eternal rest when you get to heaven but here on this earth, there is a rest from trouble because trouble doesn't last always, thank you Jesus. All you need is to do is present yourself before the full fountain that never runs dry. You must long for the refreshing that only comes from the Lord as the deer pants at the river bank, **Psalms 42:1** – As the hart panteth after the water brooks, so panteth my soul after thee, O God. As you thirst for the Lord, this fountain becomes a fountain of "Life" where you will never thirst again. Remember your Bible study, the woman by the well. She drank of the spiritual water of life, **John 4:13-14** - Jesus answered and said unto her, Whosoever drinketh of this water shall thirst again: But whosoever drinketh of the water that I shall give him shall never thirst; but the water that I shall give him shall be in him a well of water springing up into everlasting life. Jesus is telling you to, "Come", **Revelation 22:17** – And the Spirit and the bride say, Come. And let him that heareth say, Come. And let him that is athirst come. And whosoever will, let him take the water of life freely. You don't have to wait in a line to drink from this fountain and you don't have pay a dime, **Isaiah 55:1** – Ho, every one that thirsteth, come ye to the waters, and he that hath no money, come ye, buy, and eat; yea, come, buy wine and milk without money and without price. The only cost is your surrender to accept the refreshing from the Lord because the Lord is your Shepherd. Your cup will run over, freely, **Psalm 23:5** – Thou prepares a table before me in the presence of mine enemies: thou anointest my head with oil; my cup runneth over. You may have been in a dry place but the drought is over at the Fountain Gate and your cup will run over with peace, joy, and love for the God you serve, **Isaiah 58:11** – And the Lord shall guide thee continually, and satisfy thy soul in drought, and make fat thy house: and thou shalt be like a watered garden, and like a spring of water, whose waters fail not. An invitation has been given to the people of God at the Gate of the Fountain, "Come and drink from the fountain that never runs dry." Many are looking for the fountain of youth, come and drink at the Gate of the Fountain of God and your youth will be renewed. The Valley Gate can be a dry and dusty place and you will need a touch from God, **Psalm 42:2** – My soul thisteth for God, for the living God. And the Lord will come and give you the water of refreshing, **Psalm 63:1** – O God, thou art my God; early will I seek thee, my soul thirsteth for thee, my flesh longeth for thee in a dry and thirsty land, where no water is and no one can refresh you but the Word of God, Jesus. You will begin to gain strength and ready to walk in the life that the Lord has prepared for you, **Psalms 36:9** – For with thee is the fountain of life: in thy light shall we see light. At the Fountain Gate is where you are refreshed in the light of God and in your walk with the Lord who is the light of the world, **John 8:12**. At the Fountain Gate, you will need something to hold your water. Your cup will be your mind, body and soul which will run over with joy, peace and righteousness in the Holy Spirit every good and perfect gift that comes from the Lord, **James 1:17** – Every good gift and every perfect gift is from above, and cometh down from the Father of lights, with whom is no variableness, neither shadow of turning. In this world today, it is a dry place. Everything and everyone is in hurry and scrabbling to accomplish and doing and going nowhere. Watching people today will make you thirty for a fresh drink of life from the Lord as you sometimes pass through some very dry places. Sometimes on your job it seems that the air gets very thick with malice, jealousy and suspicions and everyone is against each other. Let the Word of God, Jesus, speak to you and you speak to Him, and let the water flow out and refresh you again, **Numbers 20:4** – speak unto the rock and it shall give forth his water. Always follow the direction from the Word of God for the water to flow to you. Moses did not follow God's instruction and smote the rock, **Numbers 20:11**. Never hit the Rock in disbelief. Jesus will meet you at your point of thirst and offer you the living water that you will never thirst again. Let Him speak to you each time you hear the preached Word of God and each time you open your Bible. This water is not plain water but spiritual water, **John 4:13-14** – Jesus answered

and said unto her, whosoever drinketh of this water shall thirst
again: But whosoever drinketh of the water that I shall give him
shall never thirst; but the water that I shall give him shall be in
him a well of water springing up into everlasting life. All you have
to do is believe in the Word of God to be refresh again and again,
John 7:38 – He that believeth on me, as the scripture hath said,
out of his belly shall flow rivers of living water. At the fountain,
you don't have to be greedy but you can drink until you want no
more. You will be refreshed until your cup runs over and over
again, **Psalm 23:5**. Keep your cup full of praise to Lord in
worship and honor His holy Name. You will have the right to
prosper and be in good health as your soul prospers as you drink
of the goodness of the Lord at the fountain that never runs dry.
Just know Jesus, one day you will be able to sit at the bank of the
river of heaven eternally, **Revelation 21:6** – And he said unto
me, It is done. I am Alpha and Omega, the beginning and the
end, I will give unto him that is athirst of the fountain of the water
of life freely. The shameless part of the Fountain Gate is when you
refuse the helping hand of God to relieve your thirsty soul. Never
thirst for the things of the world. You must never forget that you
are saved and never doubt your salvation. Keep you hunger and
thirst after the things of God, His Word, which is Jesus. You have
a right to drink from the wells of salvation due to time in the
Word of God, church attendance with prayer and fasting, you will
be refreshed as you sit at the feet of Jesus, **Isaiah 12:3** – Therefore
with joy shall ye draw water out of the wells of salvation. Continue
to fear the Lord, reverence Him and you will not be dry. Time
in the Word of God is the time of refreshing as you sit at the feet
of Jesus, **Isaiah 12:3** – Therefore with joy shall ye draw water

out of the wells of salvation. The wells of salvation in your soul will never run dry. You will find wisdom at the fountain, **Proverbs 18:4** – The words of a man's mouth are as deep waters, and the wellspring of wisdom as a flowing brook. Whatever sin made you travel through the Dung Gate, you will fine wisdom at the Fountain Gate. When you are refreshed in God, there is no comparison to the rest for the mind, body and soul. When you are refreshed by God at the Fountain Gate, you will find a deep respect for God. **Proverbs 14:27** – The fear of the Lord is a fountain of life, to depart from the snares of death. You will begin to love your life that is hid in Christ Jesus, **Colossians 3:1-3** – If ye then be risen with Christ, seek those things which are above, where Christ sitteth on the right hand of God. Set your affection on things above, not on things on the earth. For ye are dead, and your life is hid with Christ in God. The refreshing of the Lord keeps your mind on things that are above because you are thinking about just how "Good" the Lord has been to you. You become heavenly minded, thinking on Jesus Who is sitting on the right hand of His Father, thinking about you, as you are on this earth thinking about Him. Trust in the Lord, He will take care of His Bride, the church, **Psalm 16:1-3** - Preserve me, O God: for in thee do I put my trust. The Gate of the Fountain will flow in your all your season, summer, spring, winter and fall in all directions, **Zechariah 14:8** – And it shall be in that day, that living waters shall go out from Jerusalem; half of them toward the former sea, and half of them toward the hinder sea: in summer and in winter shall it be. Our God cannot be limited and He will not put any limits on refreshing His people. As you drink, the sun shall not smite you by day nor the moon at night, summer, under any circumstance of life, drink. Remember the woman by the well, **John 4:15** – The woman saith unto him, Sir give me this water, that I thirst not, neither come hither to draw. When you are refreshed by God, know what you are looking at, Jesus Himself. Spring up old well within my soul and make me whole. The Lord will always refresh you, **Psalm 107:35** – He turneth the wilderness into a standing water, and dry ground into water springs. You will always be refreshed by the presence of the Lord and experience the fullness of joy. This refreshing only comes from the Comforter, the Spirit of God. Stay refreshed and never allow satan to steal your joy. Remember, you were told that satan is at each gate; he never loves to see a refreshed Saint of God and wants you to bypass the Dung gate. The Dung gate is there to help you recognize and know your enemy's tactics and plan, satan. You will even recognize if the enemy is the old you. When this occurs it is time to dump the sewage at the Dung Gate.

6

The Dung Gate – Nehemiah 3:14

Satan was and never will be your friend. He is extra mad at you because he lost a soul that he thought he owned. And He will throw everything but the kitchen sink at you to slow up or even stop your growth in the Lord. Satan loves to throw his waste, which is sin, into the Christian's path. This waste is "sin". Satan wants you to transgress against the divine law of God, His Word, the Bible. This is why you can't allow the waste to become cultivated in your life; however, Jesus said, "Forgive" which allows the process to begin at the Dung Gate through repentance. Without repentance of the sin, you fail yourself and not the Lord. Failure is something that God forgives and repentance brings on the purification process in the Dung Gate. You must remember, satan is a conspirers and is in conspiracy with his plots and intriguing sins to sabotage your walk with the Lord. In the Dung Gate there is no time for negotiations with satan. Remember satan cannot do anything unless the Lord allows him and you are considered by God, **Job 3:3** – And the Lord said unto Satan, Hast thou considered by servant Job, that there is none like him in the earth, a perfect and an upright man, one that feareth God, and escheweth evil? And still he holdeth fast his integrity, although thou movedestr me against him without cause. However, also you can allow the devil to put you in the Dung Gate by your disobedience to the Word of God. This is the enemy within you. Satan wants to harm your walk with God. When you walk with satan, your walk with God will become problematic and difficult. Therefore, you end up in the Dung Gate. His sin of rebellion in heaven threw him out of heaven and now his plan is to disrupt and interfere your walk with God and keep you from reaching your heavenly home that he will never see again unless he has an audience with the Lord, **Job 1:6** – Now there was a day when the sons of God came to present themselves before the Lord, and satan came also among them. When you fall into sin, rebellion against the authority of God, you must visit the Dung Gate. This gate is the gate that you must visit, maybe once, twice or many times throughout your walk with the Lord. The Dung Gate is a gate where you can dump satan's sin and the sin that has so easily beset you, **Hebrews 12:1** – ....let us lay aside every weight, and the sin which doth so easily beset us. Sin, no matter the type causes condemnation and unpleasantness in any Christian life and if not dealt with will separate you from God. Sin separated Adam and Eve and drove them out of the presence of God, however, not from the sight of God. This is the vicinity where you can dispose of all judgments or alleged statements that satan may make against you. Satan comes to accuse you before God; however, he will be casted down, **Revelation 12:10** – And I heard a loud voice saying in heaven, Now is come salvation, and strength, and the kingdom of our God, and the power of his

Christ: for the accuser of our brethren is cast down, which accused them before our God day and night. Jesus did not come to condemn you but to save you, **John 3:17**- For God sent not his Son into the world to condemn the world; but that the world through him might be saved. Whatever has caused you to come to the Dung Gate is between you and the Lord. Satan may have the first say against you; however, the Lord has the last and final say. Yes, it may involve others, but God will take care of the situation through your end result in the gate. This sometimes is a private gate but sometimes becomes an open gate through open repentance. After you have been refreshed at the Water Fountain, satain hates you with a passion and wants to destroy your relationship with the Lord. Satan will throw everything but the kitchen at you and when he does, don't try to catch it. Just step aside and let the Lord catch whatever satan is throwing at you. Remember, satan is the accuser of the brethren, **Revelation 12:10**. Satan knows that sin in your life will slow down your growth in the Lord, to the point of serious loss, unhappiness and spiritual death. Jesus is the revealer and the disposer in the Dung Gate. He is the only One, when you call on His Name, can do by forgiveness do away with the sin that has hindered your walk with the Lord. Sin will cause you to die spiritually and loss out naturally by connecting into your life, your health and your strength. The Dung Gate is the place where sin is repented of and acceptance of the forgiveness of God is a guaranteed, **I John 1:9** – If we confess our sins, he is faithful and just to forgive us our sins, and to cleanse us from all unrighteousness. In the Old Testament the children of Israel had to make a sin offering to the Lord, **Exodus 29:14** – But the flesh of the bullock, and his skin, and his dung, shalt thou burn with fire without the camp: it is a sin offering. Now, all we have to do is "come" to Jesus, Jesus is the only garbage collector that can get rid of sin that is garbage in the Christian life today. In the Dung Gate, talk to the Lord and don't try to justify your sin or blame someone else, **Isaiah 1:18** – Come let us reason together, saith the Lord: though your sins be as scarlet, they shall be as white as snow; though they be red like crimson, they shall be as wool. God is ready to forgive in Jesus' Name; just repent in Jesus' Name. All you have to do is cast that sin upon Jesus because He cares for you, **I Peter 5:7**. Through all the mistakes, God loves you. All sin, past, present and future sins were nailed and forgiven at the Cross of Calvary to show God is a sovereign God with all power in His powerful capable hands in every situation in your life. You must recognize the sovereignty of God and he will forgive you in the Dung Gate. The Lord will accept your sin offering because He is faithful and just to forgive because His promises of His covenant. Never forget the covenant of God, from Abraham to you, and it is an everlasting covenant, **Ezekiel 37:26**. Sin does not break God's covenant it just offers forgiveness when you confess your sins. The Dung Gate stinks because sin stinks in the nose of God. When satan comes along, don't talk to him, tell him, "you stink" and your stench will not remain around you because you must submit this horrible smell to God and the unpleasant odor, satan, will go, **James 4:7** – Submit yourselves therefore to God. Resist the devil, and he will free from you. No matter what the sin, God wants you to humble yourself and He will forgive you, **James 4:8** and lift you up where you belong. Jesus is the only One who forgives you of your sins and He is the only One Who can forgive you when you fall, **II Corinthians 5:21** – For he hath made him to be sin for us, who knew no sin; that we might be made the righteousness of God in him. Failures in you are when you know to do well and you do not do it, **James 4:17** - Therefore to him that knoweth to do good, and doeth it not; to him it is sin, however, you still must go to the Lord and ask for forgiveness. If you don't repent, then you go to the Dung Gate to get rid of the sin that so easily beset you, **Hebrews 12:1**. Satan will follow you into the Dung Gate. The smell of sin does not bother him because he is the Father of lies, **John 8:44** and wants to keep you confused and keep you thinking that you can't rid of the sin and shame that has occurred. The Lord is your strength, **Psalm 73:26**, you may have fallen down but you must get back up again. The Lord is waiting to renew you and take you back to the Water Gate to bathe as you repent, **Hebrews 6:6**. Never let the smell of condemnation keep you in the Dung Gate. Just like a dog, satan will track you when you wrap yourself in condemnation but you are proved by God when you repent, **Romans 8:1**. Satan hates you when your mind is made up to serve the Lord no matter the cost. Satan works in two areas, your mind and your flesh, **Galatians 5:17** – For the flesh lusteth against the Spirit, and the Spirit against the flesh and these are contrary the one to the other: so that ye cannot do the things that ye would. The conflict begins in your mind first in what you think about concerning the body and the things of the world. This is why we must have the mind of Christ and the flesh must be crucified, **Galatians 5:24** – And they that are Christ's have crucified the flesh with the affections and lusts, only by the Word of God. Temptations of this world is getting more and more of a sin in the people of God today, however, the Lord promises us to deliver us from temptations that are evil, **Matthew 6:13**. Watching so called Christian reality shows will cause damage to your walk with God. They are not real but as you line it up with the Word of God you will see the falseness, fakeness and the evilness displayed against the Word of God. Don't let temptation drive you into the Dung Gate, **II Corinthians 10:13**, the Lord in His Word will make a way of escape. There are so many stumbling blocks in the world today and has ended up in the church. Remember, yield not to temptation, for yielding is sin. Satan loves to accuse the men and women of God and bring up the past and even the present to accuse you before the Lord, **Revelation 12:10** - .....for the accuser of our brethren is cast down, which accused them before our God day and night. Today you may have made a mistake, repent, and just let satan continue to talk because the Lord has forgiven you, **Hebrews 4:14** – Seeing then that we have a great high priest, that is passed unto the heavens, Jesus the Son of God, let us hold fast our profession and you shall never be moved from the forgiveness of the Lord. Just let satan continues to accuse you of your past but your past the Lord does not remember, **Isaiah 43:25** – I, even I, am he that blotteth out thy transgressions for mine own sake, and will not remember thy sins. Because of repentance, your sins have been washed away, **I John 1:9** – If we confess our sins, he is faithful and just to forgive us our sins, and to cleanse us from all unrighteousness. Satan cannot hold any sin over your head, you are forgiven. In the Dung Gate you can tell satan to take his packages of deceit and sin back to the dust where he and it belongs. You have to walk as a child of God and talk like a child of God and submit yourself to the Lord, resist the devil and he will flee from you. You don't have to accept anything from hell's gate, just send it back to sender, satan. Just keep the mind of Christ and forget those things that are behind you and reach forward for the things that are in Christ Jesus and step out of the Dung Gate. You may have to return again, repent, let go and let the Lord led you onward and forward to perfection that can only be found in Jesus Christ. Yes, the Dung Gate is a very smelly place. What is Dung? Natural dung is droppings, feces, manure, or just a very smelly substance. Dung is the excrement of man or beast. Dung is not usable to man or beast but is good for nothing. Spiritually, Dung is sin. Dung represents sin in a person's life and you must go to the Dung Gate deposit and remember it no more. Sin always stinks. Sin truly stinks to the person who know to do well and does it not, **James 4:17** - Therefore to him that knoweth to do good, and doeth it not, to him it is sin. When an individual is confessing Jesus Christ he or she should not be found in the dung gate. However, the Lord will allow you to get here so that you can put whatever is wasting your time and energy to rest here at the dung gate. This is the place where you can dispose of rubbish, garbage and dung. In layman's terms, everything that is not like the Lord. God is the only One who can turn Dung into something "good". Just like the prodigal son, he was in the dung gate with pigs and came to himself, repented and returned back to his father's house, **Luke 15:11-32**. The prodigal son lost all to gain more from his father. The same with a child of God, you will gain and not lose your reward waiting for you in heaven. The Dung Gate is where you get rid of waste that is stopping your growth in God and whatever is detrimental to your soul. Sin causes you to feel guilty and condemned. Sin's main goal is to separate you from the love of God and make you feel that God does not love you. In the Dung Gate, there is always plenty to learn and do to get the feelings of the Dung Gate. The Dung Gate is the dumping stage. When God made the human body it was marvelously made, **Psalms 139:14**, to get rid of waste and it is same with the spiritual body. The Lord with His ultimate wisdom allows the natural body to release waste; we must have a release in the spiritual body which is sin, the weight and the sins that so easily beset us, **Hebrews 12:1** – Wherefore seeing we also are compassed about with so great a cloud of witnesses, let us lay aside every weight, and the sin which doth so easily beset us, and let us run with patience the race that is set before us. The Bible is a complete book of witnesses that made mistakes but continued to follow the God of Abraham, Isaac and Jacob, the True and Living God. Moses killed a man and lived on the backside of the desert but dumped and became the pastor of pastors that led millions of people toward the Promised Land. King David also killed a man but he dumped and became the man after God's own heart. Jonah had to dump the spirit of disobedience and saved a whole city after that repented. Every witness in the Word of God, we all can learn the lesson and learn to dump in the Name of Jesus, **vs 2** – Looking unto Jesus the author and finisher of our faith; who for the job that was set before him endured the cross, despising the shame, and is set down at the right hand of the throne of God. Dumping is done at the altar of repentance. Repentance is not to embarrass you but to make you strong in the Lord as you learn the ways of the Lord, **Psalm 119:26-28** – I have declared my ways, and thou heardest me" teach me thy statutes. Make me to understand the way of thy precepts, so shall I talk of thy wondrous works. My soul melteth for heaviness" strengthen thou me according unto thy word. Again, the Lord will renew you and your faith will be restored because satan has lie and spoke that you failed God and God's love is no longer yours but always remember, "satan is a liar." You can and will be restored, **Hebrews 6:6** – If they shall fall away, to renew them again unto repentance; seeing they crucify to themselves the Son of God afresh, and put him to an open shame. When you sin, you are put to shame not Jesus and it is impossible to crucify Him again but He only died once, **Hebrews 9:28** – So Christ was once offered to bear the sins of many; and unto them that look for him shall he appear the second time without sin unto salvation. Jesus said it only once on the cross, "It is finished" and He did not repeat Himself, once is enough for the cost of redemption. You are dead to sin and have the grace of God upon your life, **Romans 6:1-2** – What shall we say then? Shall we continue in sin, that grace may abound? God forbid. How shall we, that are dead to sin, live any longer there in? Continuously remember that the Dung Gate is where you send everything that the devil has tried to do to you back to satan. Never confront the devil, Jesus has already confronted him for you by the Cross of Calvary and the sample of His temptation in the wilderness. You just each time rely on the Word of God, Jesus, and tell satan, "It is Written." Again, submit yourself to God, resist the devil and you will see satan flee from you. Because of your faith and your confidence in the Lord and what He did at the Cross of Calvary you faith is built in the Dung Gate. Jesus defeated the devil; never let the devil defeat you. Repent, forgive yourself, and continue to walk with the Lord. So, as you walk toward the exit of the Dung Gate, tell that devil, "It is finished." Now, let go to the Water Gate for a good bath and say like King David, **Psalm 51:7** – Pure me with hyssop, and I shall be clean: wash me, and I shall be whiter than snow. This is done only by the Spirit of God, the Holy Ghost. Dung Gate may have done a job on you; however, let's go into the Water Gate and bathe and take the grave clothes off and experience the new life again.

7

The Water Gate – Nehemiah 3:26

In churches today, there are vessels of honor and dishonor and the Lord knows those who are His, **II Timothy 2:20-21**. The Lord wants to use His church to draw the world to Him. Therefore, you must bathe in the Word of God to be fit to be used by the Lord. Moses had to bathe Aaron and his sons before they entered into the priestly dues, **Leviticus 16:20** - You must know that when you bathe naturally, you are not thoroughly cleansed but when you bathe in the Word of God, you are thoroughly cleansed because of Jesus Christ, **Ephesians 5:26**. Water in the Word of God represents the Holy Ghost. The Holy Ghost is the power of God that works on the inside and shows forth on the outside and makes a change in your life. John said that he baptized the people in water but there is one that cometh that will baptize you with the Holy Ghost, **John 1:26**. In the Water Gate, you must experience the baptism of your soul, from head to foot, immersed into water, **Romans 6:3-4** – Know ye not, that so many of us as were baptized into Jesus Christ were baptized into his death? Therefore we are buried with him by baptism into death: that like as Christ was raised up from the dead by the glory of the Father, even so we also should walk in newness of life. Water baptism gives you newness of life. Just as Jesus is our example, we must follow Him just as He was baptized. The Water Gate is where you are bathed in the love of God and reminded of His love for you. Children or babies are sprinkles but as an adult, you are immersed in the water and God will sprinkle you, **Ezekiel 36:25** – Then will I sprinkle clean water upon you, and ye shall be clean: from all your filthiness, and from all your idols, will I cleanse you. The devil is always and will always be the accuser of the church, **Revelation 12:10**. The enemy, satan, will one day be put in chains and casted into hell to trouble the church no more, **Revelation 20:10**. At the Water Gate continue to consecrate yourself by the Word of God in your mind and in your heart. Keep your mind on Christ and let the mind of Christ be in you, **Philippine 2:5**, because the mind of Christ is a terrible thing to waste. The mind of Christ in the Water Gate will give you instructions to "go wash" and obedience is the key in the Water Gate. In the Old Testament, God told Naaman to "go wash" in the Jordan River seven times, **II Kings 5:10**. He would have not recovered from the leprosy that was affecting his life. When you disobey the command to go wash, you will die spiritually because you fail to wash away things that are not the will of God in your life. Cigarettes generate cancer. Alcohol causes deterioration of the liver. Over eating brings on self-pity. In the New Testament, Jesus told the man to go and wash in the Pool of Siloam to be cured from his blindness. The Lord wants you to see clear and to wash at the Water Gate when necessary, **Psalm 146:8**. When you bathe, most of the time you bathe alone. However, sometimes in the Water Gate you have to go to the altar in your church and stay there until you go deep down into the water prepared by the Holy Ghost. You immerge deep down into the Word of God, return back to your first love, Jesus Christ with open repentance from your heart and this is good for the soul, **Isaiah 1:18**. After a furious battle with satan, you need to be refreshed and restored at the Water Gate. You must look at the Word of God for your refreshing. The Bible, sixty-six books with two sections, Old and New Testaments gives us all that we need for abiding in the Water Gate, **II Timothy 3:16** – All scripture is given by inspiration of God, and is profitable for doctrine, for reproof, for correction, for instruction in righteousness. There are no exceptions when it comes to the Bible. The Water Gate is where the Word of God washes you all over from the top of your head to the soul of your feet. We cannot pick and choose what scripture we should wash with because the Word of God must be applied to every aspects of your life. When you wash you use your soap, body wash, hand towel, brush, and all the items necessary to completely obtain the maximum cleansing. Sometimes you have to do a complete wash over again if necessary. God told the prophet Ezekiel to eat the whole roll, **Ezekiel 3:1** – Moreover he said unto me, Son of man, eat that thou fondest; eat this roll, and go speak unto the house of Israel and the Lord is telling the church today, "Read, study and apply the Word of God to our lives today and don't be ashamed to wash, **Romans 1:16** – For I am not ashamed of the gospel of Christ: for it is the power of God unto salvation to everyone that believeth, to the Jew first, and also to the Greek. In the Old Testament, God required His people to make the difference in the world because they were His people. However, they could not make the difference between clean and unclean and holy and unholy, **Jeremiah 2:21-22** – Yet I had planted thee a noble vine, wholly a right seed: how then art thou turned into the degenerate plant of a strange vine unto me? For though thou wash thee with nitre, and take thee much soap, yet thine iniquity is marked before me, saith the Lord God. This is the reason Jesus had to die for the sins of the world, we could not cleanse ourselves. In the Sheep Gate, you as you read Matthew, Mark, Luke and John, you know how Jesus has called you and in the Water Gate, you will realize how Jesus will wash you and deliver you and keep you. Jesus said, **Luke 4:18-19** – The Spirit of the Lord is upon me, because he hath anointed me to preach the gospel to the poor; he hath sent me to heal the brokenhearted, to preach deliverance to the captives, and recovering of sight to the blind, to set at liberty them that are bruised. To preach the acceptable year of the Lord. The people of God, the church, must accept the whole Bible in the Water Gate to be sanctified. Many want the anointing of God in their lives but you cannot be anointed with sanctification first. The anointing is not the anointing to sing or even preach. The anointing comes with full dedication to the Lord in the Water Gate. You cannot reject the Old Testament because you feel that it is outdated. God's word is up to date no matter what century, year or day, **Romans 14:5** – For whatsoever things were written aforetime were written for our learning, that we through patience and comfort of the scriptures might have hope. You must learn the Old Testament stories and the New Testament doctrines, principles and the words that Jesus spoke. The most notable is the parables; the stories that are earthly with a heavenly meaning. Also remember all scriptures are given for your benefit. The Word of God will profit you; help you grow in the doctrine, requirements and for correction and instruction in righteousness. Reading the whole Old Testament shows the love of God and the wrath of God. The New Testament shows the Love of God through His Son, Jesus Christ, **John 3:16** – For God so loved the world, that he gave his only begotten Son, that whosoever believeth in him should not perish, but have everlasting life. As you process through the Water Gate, the Lord will be there from the beginning to the ending. The Word of God shows you what God can do for His people, from the beginning, **Genesis 1:1** – In the beginning God to **John 1:1** – In the beginning was the Word, and the Word was with God, and the Word was God. As you refresh in the Water Gate, all three are there to cleanse you and keep you. God is there from the very beginning. Jesus is there because of the Word of God. Also, the Holy Ghost is there to comfort you, **John 16:7** – Nevertheless I tell you the truth; It is expedient for you that I go away: for if I go not away the Comforter will not come unto you: but if I depart, I will send him unto you. As you consecration and dedicate yourself in the Water Gate, you will be very happy that the Comforter, the Holy Spirit of God, has come into your life. As you walk through the many elements of the Water Gate, you will begin to know that God can do anything but fail, **Jeremiah 32:17** – Ah, Lord God! Behold, thou hast made the heaven and the earth by thy great power and stretched out arm, and there is nothing too hard for thee and gives the people of God encouragement in the time of trouble, **Psalm 46:1** – God is our refuge and strength, a very present help in the time of trouble. Whatever you feel is separating you from the love of God can be taken away at the Water Gate. Any fear, doubt, and frustration that want to separate you from the love of God can be washed away upon your prayer, **Psalm 51:2** – Wash me thoroughly from mine iniquity, and cleanse me from my sin. You must acknowledge any sin in the Water Gate to be cleansed from sin. David wanted the cleansing of the Lord from the inside out, **Psalm 51:6** – Behold, thou desirest truth in the inward parts: and in the hidden part thou shalt make me to know wisdom. In the Water Gate, you will be cleansing from parts that nobody can see but God. Now that is a cleansing! Remember Peter; ask the Lord to wash you all over, **John 13:8-9** – Peter saith unto him, Thou shalt never wash my feet. Jesus answered him, If I wash thee not, thou hast no part with me. Simon Peter saith unto him, Lord not my feet only, but also my hands and my head. You will see the difference in yourself once you have experience the Water Gate sanctification. You will tell the world that ivory soap did not cleanse you and bleach did not take away the stain of sin from your life. In the Water Gate your request will be the request of the King's kid, **Psalm 51:7** – Purge me with hyssop, and I shall be clean: wash me, and I will be whiter than snow. At the Water Gate because of the Spirit of God within you, God's business becomes your business. You desire to do the will of God and let the Will of God be done in your life, **John 6:38-40** – For I came down from heaven, not to do mine own will, but the will of him that sent me. **Act 8**, Philip met the Ethiopian at the Water Gate and the Ethiopian's business became the God in Philip's business. At the Water Gate, God give direction. You must develop an ear to hear and a spirit to do what God instructs for you to do, **Acts 8:26** - And the angel of the Lord spake unto Philip saying, Arise, and go toward the south unto the way that goeth down from Jerusalem unto Gaza, which is desert. Philip was in the city of Samaria and many were cleansed from unclean spirit and brought great joy, revival in the city of Samaria, **Acts 8:5-8**. Philip had to get to the Water Gate as directed by the Lord. Many preachers today get tired fast but the Water Gate will keep you busy for the Lord. God did not give further instruction to Philip, He just told him to arise with His direction and it was in a desert. The Holy Ghost, the Spirit of God, wants to do a work in your life in the Water Gate. The Holy Ghost wants to lead you and guide you in all truths and this cannot be done outside the Word of God. God's Word a lamp unto your feet and a light unto your path especially when you become sanctified by the Word of God, **John 17:17** – Sanctify them through thy truth: thy word is truth. Sanctify means to be cleaned by the Word of God. The Word of God must have an effect in our lives. The Word of God will give you provision and God's word does not return unto Him void, **Isaiah 55:10-11** – For as the rain cometh down, and the snow from heaven, and returned not thither, but watered the earth, and make it bring forth and bud, that it may give seed to the sower, and bread to the eater: So shall my word be that go forth out of my mouth: it shall not return unto me void, but it shall accomplish that which I please, and it shall prosper in the thing whereto I sent it. In the Water Gate the people of God rely and trust in the Word of God and His name is Jesus. At the Water Gate the church must be sanctified by the Word of God. Many feel that the pastors only and those called to the five-fold ministry, prophets, teachers, apostles, evangelists but from the pulpit out the door must be sanctified, **Ephesians 5:26** – That he might sanctify and cleanse it with the washing of water by the Word. The Water Gate was located next to the fountain gate. Sometimes you will need to be washed and often times you will have needed to be refreshed. For our lives, God puts everything in order and all we can say is "It is good." There are three doctrines of the church that you must partake of with this great salvation, the Lord's Supper, Feet Washing and Water Baptism. When you partake of the Lord's Supper, you show forth your faith and that you believe in what Jesus accomplished on the Cross of Calvary. When you partake of Feet Washing, you show the newness in your life. You are baptized to demonstrate to the world that you are no longer in darkness and that you believe in Jesus' death, burial and resurrection, **Colossians 2:12-13** – Buried with him in baptism, wherein also ye are risen with him through the faith of the operation of God, who hath raised him from the dead. And you, being dead in your sins and the uncircumcision of our flesh, hath he quickened together with him having forgiven you all trespasses. At the Water Gate, your praise belong only to God, **Jude 25** – Now unto him that is able to keep you from falling, and to present you faultless before the presence of his glory with exceeding joy, to the only wise God our Savior, be glory and majesty, dominion and power, both now and ever. Amen. You are now clean and walking with the Lord with your hands in His hand. You are feeling confident and happy. Stay clean in the eyesight of the Lord, **Galatians 2:20** – I am crucified with Christ: nevertheless I live; yet not I, but Christ liveth in me: and the life which I now live in the flesh I live by the faith of the Son of God, who loved me, and gave himself for me. Now it is time to be inspected by the Lord in the Inspection Gate.

8

The Inspection Gate –
Nehemiah 3:31

Grandmothers are the best inspectors after their grandchild has taken a bath. She looks behind the ears and even to the point of smelling the armpits. Also, the Lord comes down and inspects His people by His Word, **Hebrews 4:13**. This is called a visitation from the Lord. We serve a God that neither sleeps nor slumbers and His eyes go throughout the whole earth beholding the good and the evil. When you are drafted into the armed forces, you find out that you don't know anything and what you did know has to come unto subjection to the authorities over you. No matter if you are an officer or an enlisted member of the armed forces, you must obey those that have the rule over you, **Hebrews 13:17**. The authorities in the Inspection Gate are God, the Father, the Son, Jesus Christ and the Holy Ghost, the Spirit of God. Remember, just one General to answer to, God, **Deuteronomy 6:4** - Hear, O Israel: the Lord our God is one Lord and the authority and the power belongs to God, **Psalm 62:11**. At the Inspection Gate, you realize that you are in the army of the Lord,

Joel 2:11 – And the Lord shall utter his voice before his army: for his camp is very great: for he is strong that executeth is world: for the day of the Lord is great and very terrible; and who can abide it? You begin to march to a different drum and you are ready for any inspection when the Lord calls for you to be inspected, **Matthew 24:44** – Therefore be ye also ready for in such an hour as y think not the Son of man cometh. It is hard to pass an inspection, especially when you are not ready. The Word of God helps you to prepare yourself in the inspection Gate. The Word of God, your Bible, is the book to give yourself a pre-inspection. Grandmothers are the best inspectors of their grandchildren after they have taken a bath from the top of the head to the small little toes. Grandma checks your ears, under the arms, feet and toes and even sometimes the private areas of the body. The Inspection Gate is just where you to come and be inspected by the Word of God, **Psalm 17:3** – Thou hast proved mine heart; thou hast visited me in the night; thou hast tried me, and shalt find nothing; I am purposed that my mouth shall not transgress. God came down to inspect His creation, man, **Genesis 6**. Mankind began to increase on the face of the earth. God was displeased with mankind and only one man did not fail the inspection. His name was Noah. Noah passed the inspection because he found grace in the eyes of the Lord and was saved from the flood that the Lord used to destroy corruption upon the earth. God remembered Noah just as He will remember you on the judgment day. The first thing for passing God's inspection is to find grace in His sight. Again, the Lord came down to inspect man after the flood, **Genesis 11**. Man was trying to build a city and a tower that may reach into heaven and wanted to make them a name for themselves. The humility of man was corrupted in the eyesight of God again. God did not destroy man because of His promise, His Word. The Lord scattered mankind throughout the face of the earth and confounded their language. This is why we have nations and different languages throughout the earth. This is why we must come to the Inspection Gate because God is coming again to inspect His people and to judge the world. The church today, the people of God need to come into the Inspection Gate to see if they are in working order and working condition. God is a good God and He is concerned with the condition of His people and Jesus is concerned about His body, the church. In invitation to the Inspection Gate is "Come", **Isaiah 1:18** – Come now, and let us reason together, saith the Lord: though your sins be as scarlet, they shall be as white as snow; though they be red like crimson, they shall be as wool. There will be a time to come to Jesus and have an inspection or just a talk between you and the Chief Shepherd of your soul, **I Peter 5:5**. A shepherd examines his sheep to keep parasites out of their wool, nose, ears, or eyes. This keeps the sheep from going mad due to the irritation caused by the parasites. You go through a review in the military to see how you are adapting to military life. The Lord inspects His people to help them get ready for that great day, the coming of the Lord. You will one day stand before the judgment seat of Christ, **II Corinthians 5:10**. The Inspection Gate is where you allow the Word of God to examine you before you are judged by the Lord. You must allow the Word of God to inspect the fruits that are growing as you walk with the Lord. Are they real or fake fruit? You must always remember that the Lord is a fruit inspector. The Fruits of the Spirit is the first stage that we ourselves can inspect, **Galatians 5:22-23** – But the fruit of the Spirit is love, joy, peace, longsuffering, gentleness, goodness, faith, meekness, temperance: against such there is no law. As you are in the Inspection Gate, the Lord looks at your spiritual sprits daily. The natural shepherd calls the sheep in to be inspected for parasites and bugs that maybe entangled in the sheep's wool. The Lord inspects His sheep for any sin that may have so easily beset them and must be inspected at the Inspection Gate. After all, the Lord is coming back for a church that is without a spot or a wrinkle, **Ephesian 5:26-27** – That he might sanctify and cleanse it with the washing of water by the word. That he might present it to himself a glorious church, not having spot or wrinkle, or any such thing: but that it should be holy and without blemish. At the Lord's Inspection Gate, the manual used by the Lord is His Word, the Bible. Any solider in the natural Armed Forces have manuals that they must read to get ready for inspections from their superior officers. Before any inspection, you must read and be examined by the Word of God and nothing else, with no exception. The Word of God applies to all of the Lord's sheep. This Inspection Gate will let you know if you are compromising the Word of God with your walk with God. Jesus, the Good Shepherd, gave His life at the Cross of Calvary, died and rose again for your justification that you can be presented faultless and blameless, **Colossians 1:22** – In the body of his flesh through death, to present you holy, and unblameable, and unreproveable in his sight. Satan will be unable to accuse you because you have passed the inspection of the Good Shepherd, Jesus Christ. If you did not pass the inspection, you may have to go back to the Dung Gate. On this earth you will be judged by man but man does not have a heaven or a hell to put eternally. The Inspection Gate is where you cross examining yourself by the Word of God for your spiritual well-being. No matter how much you tell yourself, "I'm OK", there is always room for an examination from the Lord who is the righteous judge. The Lord's examination will do you no harm. You will be checked for any sin that may have easily beset you, **Hebrews 12:1**. You must know that it is the hidden things of the heart that the Lord must examine because the heart is very deceitful, **Jeremiah 17:9**. Your inspection or examination has the best examiner and physician and His Name is Jesus, **Exodus 15:3**. Your examination has the best regulation or medical book and it is the Bible, **Hebrews 4:12**. The Word of God will cut but it will heal whatever the examiner sees and finds and Jesus is His Name. The analysis and prognosis will be outstanding will a great bill of health and wealth because the Word of God will not return to Him void, **Isaiah 55:11**. Your spiritual outcome will have a great outcome because you will be in good health even as your soul prospers in Christ Jesus. The Inspection Gate on this earth helps you to get ready for the final inspection at the judgment seat of Christ for the people of God, the church. Pass the inspection as you are inspected by the Word of God and you will hear, well done good and faithful servant, **Matthew 25:23**. These Words at the end inspection you do not want to hear, "Depart from Me (Jesus) you worker of iniquity, I know you not, **Matthew 7:23**. The final inspection will let you know where your eternal home will be, heaven or hell. Listen to the while guidance of the Holy Ghost and the direction given by the Word of God and the inspection gate will be your friend and not your enemy. Remember, God's Word makes no mistakes as you regard and follow His Word without compromise. The Lord has assigned His five-fold ministry to help you inspect your fruits by the Word, **Ephesians 4:11-12** – And he gave some apostles, and some, prophets; and some evangelists, and some pastors and teachers; for the perfecting of the saints, for the work of the ministry, for the edifying of the body of Christ. As you listen to the Word of God, through your pastor, visiting evangelists, Bible teachers, visiting prophets and apostles, they can help you even if they step on your toes by the Word of God. The Spirit of God will get into your personal business and clean your house. All inspections must be taken seriously. In God's inspection, **I Corinthians 3:13** – Every man's work shall be made manifest: for the day shall declare it, because it shall be revealed by fire; and the fire shall try every man's work of what sort it is. This inspection brings everything to the light, the Light of God, Jesus Christ. God's inspection involves fire that will burn up everything that is not like God. After the Inspection Gate, you are ready to faith the good fight of faith, **I Timothy 6:12** – Fight the good fight of faith, lay hold on eternal life, whereunto thou art also called, and hast professed a good profession before many witnesses. With checks and balances complete, now you are ready to enter into the Horse Gate.

The Horse Gate – Nehemiah 3:28

When you step into the Horse Gate the Spirit of God overpowers you. The presence of God's authority is obvious. There is no space for the carnal mind because the carnal mind can receive nothing from the Lord pertaining to the Spirit of God, **I Corinthians 2:14**. All your guidelines will be given by the Word of God and your marching orders will come from the Spirit of God. This gate is ruled by the Spirit of God and is full of the power of God. You have passed your inspection and now ready to fight the good fight of faith in the Horse Gate. You must be solider ready to engage in war against the wiles of the devil, **Ephesians 6:11**. There is no hesitation and no delays; you are just "Ready." This gate represents and manifests the "Power" of God in your life, the overcoming power of the Holy Ghost. With determination toward victory no matter the cost, obeying the Word of God and not the standards of the world, **Acts 5:29** – Then Peter and the other apostles answered and said, We ought to obey God rather than men. You will win the battle engaged against satan no matter the uncontrollable conditions that is beyond your control and trying to make you a victim of circumstance. The Horse Gate represents the battle that you see in the natural and it becomes a spiritual battle, **Ephesians 6:12** – For we wrestle not against flesh and blood, but against principalities, against powers, against the rulers of the darkness of the world, against spiritual wickedness in high places. This is a gate that shows the maturity of the Christian and has accepted and follows Jesus Christ. This individual mounts a beautiful horse. The striking appearance of that person as he or she mounts stands in beauty. We, in the Horse Gate, stand in the beauty of holiness, **Psalms 95:6**. The horse stands at attention waiting for the command of the rider, you. Bow down in prayer each day before you ride into the battle of the day. Success in the battle will not be yours without skill in the Word of God concerning prayer and fasting. This warfare is in prayer, intercessory prayer and fasting which pull down strongholds in your life and as you go into battle for others, **II Corinthians 10:3-5** – For though we walk in the flesh, we do not war after the flesh: for the weapons of our warfare are not carnal, but mighty through God to the pulling down of strong holds;) casting down imaginations and high thing that exalteth itself against the knowledge of God, and bringing into captivity every thought to the obedience of Christ. This gate is an exciting gate because you can see the very movement of God through prayer and fasting in a believer's life and in the life of other believers. Everyone loves a fast horse, just ask those who go to the horse races. This race that all believers are involved with is the race to eternal life. This gate keeps you on the move for Jesus against satan and every principalities of darkness. The Horse Gate represents warfare. Daily, you must keep yourself groomed in the Word of God which is sharper than any two edged sword, **Hebrews 4:12** which is the sword of the Spirit, which is the Word of God, **Ephesians 6:17**. You are never bored in the Horse Gate because there is always something to do to keep yourself prepared for battle. The Horse Gate gauges your strength to perform whatever task the Lord requires you to achieve. This task you must accomplish with certainty. Never get in a hurry, **I Corinthians 9:24, 26**. You will quickly learn that it is not by power, your power, and not by strength, your strength but by the Spirit of the Lord, **Zechariah 4:6**. Each day, you realize that you are not going on your own power or strength and that you must rely on the strength of God. Remember David, he did not know that day he would destroy the giant Goliath. He was prepared by killing a bear and a lion that wanted to destroy his father's sheep. David remembered his responsibility to his household. David did not back down in fear. He stood his ground and gained the victory over the giant. Any giant can be defeated when you ride out of the Horse Gate in the proper manner with no fear or doubt and your enemy will be delivered into your hands. The Horse Gate is a beautiful sight in a church when the church is governed by the power of the Holy Ghost. The people of God are peculiar to the world because of their strength in believing the God they serve. The entire congregation is at attendance and ready to go into battle at the sound of the trumpet because they are a chosen people, a royal priesthood, a holy nation that shows forth the praises of God in their attitude, life style and demeanor, **I Peter 2:9**. In the Horse Gate you are fully obedient and loyal because you are chosen to run this race toward the high calling in Christ Jesus, **Philippians 3:14**. In the Horse Gate you do not let the devil make you lame. Naturally, a lame horse has to be shot but spiritually you will have to be restored. You do not walk uneven or become disabled to finish the race because your spiritual horse is weak, **Psalm 33:17** – A horse is a vain thing for safety: neither shall he deliver any by his great strength. When you need more power seek the Lord. **Psalm 147:10-11** – He delighteth not in the strength of the horse: he taketh not pleasure in the legs of a man. The Lord taketh pleasure in them that fear him, in those that hope in his mercy. God was not impressed with Solomon's horses, **I Kings 4:26** – And Solomon had forty thousand stalls of horses for his chariots, and twelve thousand horsemen. Wisdom is the key with knowledge in God's ability for your ability in the Horse Gate. The rider must have the same strength and endurance as the horse he/she is riding naturally; same as spiritually. The next key to a successful ride is obedience. In the Horse Gate, keep the Word of God in your mouth and hide the Word of God in your heart and your horse will not run wild, **Psalm 32:9** – Be ye not as the horse, or as the mule, which have no understanding: whose mouth must be held in with bit and bridle, lest they come near unto thee. **James 3:3-4** – Behold, we put bits in the horses' mouths, that they may obey us; and we turn about their whole body. Behold also the ships, which though they be so great, and are driven of fierce winds, yet are they turned about with a very small helm, whithersoever the governor listeth. Keep an understanding of your position in the Horse Gate and keep your body under subjection, **I Corinthians 9:27** – But I keep under my body, and bring it into subjection: lest that by any means, when I have preached to others, I myself should be a castaway. In the Horse Gate, the flesh cannot rule. Horses are strong; in order to ride to victory, you must be strong. In the last days, in the Horse Gate, you will see many horses. As you grow in the knowledge of the Lord, you will recognize these horses as spiritual horses galloping throughout the earth today. Whatever is happening in the news today, in the church and even in your family, you must recognize these various horses. You will see a black horse which represent the lack in the land, **Revelations 6:5-6** – And when he had opened the third seal, I heard the third beast say, Come and see. And I beheld, and lo a black horse; and he that sat on him had a pair of balances in his hand. And I heard a voice in the midst of the four beasts say, A measure of wheat for a penny, and three measures of barley for a penny; and see thou hurt not the oil and the wine. As you ride and observe the economy and businesses closing remember the Word of God, **Psalm 37:25** – I have been young, and now am old; yet have I not seen the righteous forsaken, nor his seed begging bread. Keep planting seeds of righteousness because the seed is blessed. Your concern must always be focused on your horse and the "One" Who rides the white horse, **Revelations 6:2** – And I saw, and behold a white horse: and he that sat on him had a bow; and a crown was given unto him: and he went forth conquering, and to conquer. Always remember in these last days, "You Win" all because of Jesus, **Romans 8:37** – Nay, in all these things we are more than conquerors through him that loved us. And His Name is Jesus, **Revelations 19:11, 16** – And I saw heaven opened, and behold a white horse; and he that was upon him was called Faithful and True, and in righteousness he doth judge and make war. And he hath on his vesture and on his thigh a name written, KING OF KINGS, AND LORD OF LORDS. Continue to ride your horse in righteousness and seek after the truth of every situation, one day you will ride in the army of the Lord to bring war upon your enemy, **Revelations 19:14** – And the armies which were in heaven followed him (Jesus) upon white horses, clothed in fine linen, white and clean. Stay faithful to the power of God in your life. Don't misuse this power that God has given you in the Horse Gate that you one day will return back with Jesus Christ to reign forever and forever. You will see a red horse, **Revelations 6:4** – And there went out another horse that was red: and power was given to him that sat thereon to take peace from the earth, and that they should kill one another: and there was given unto him a great sword. In the last days, wars will break out, **Matthew 24:6** – And ye shall hear of wars and rumors of wars: see that ye be not troubled. You must keep your peace and stay under the redeeming power of the Blood of Jesus, the One who rides the white horse and His name is Jesus. Stay upon your horse relying on the mercy of the Lord and remember there is redemption and redeeming power in the Blood of Jesus. Remember the peace that only the Lord gives, **Philippians 4:7** – And the peace of God, which passeth all understanding, shall keep your hearts and minds through Christ Jesus. You know that because of your love for Jesus, you will be adequate and effective that the devil runs away from you as you run to God for rest and refreshing, **James 4:7**. You will feel the brushing of your cares away and your oats will not be wild oats but will come from the Word of God for nourishment to run race after race after race. It may be the race to help someone along the way. There will be two riders on the horse and you won't mind because you have brought a wounded solider back to the Horse Gate. The Lord has a great army of soldiers that will return with Him back to earth to judge mankind one day. Remember as you ride on through victory after victory, every eye shall see Him (Jesus) and every tongues will confess on that day. The best part is to see Jesus, the Lord of Hosts, **Luke 21:27** – And then shall they see the Son of man coming in a cloud with power and great glory. Keep confessing and looking for Jesus' return as you stay in the Army of the Lord. Remember, you will always have one more battle to fight in God's army. Stay mounted, ready for battle and ride with authority over the wiles of satan as a solider in the Army of the Lord. Now that you have learned to be a solider, now it is time to learn to be a prisoner in the Prison Gate.

10

The Prison Gate – Nehemiah 3:1, 32

You have gone from becoming a sheep, to a witness, to a solider, and now you are prisoner of the Lord, captured by the Love of Jesus. With your hands lifted up and your mouth filled with praise and with a heart of thanksgiving, you are now a prisoner, **Psalm 63:4** – Thus will I bless thee while I live: I will lift up my hands in thy name. A prisoner is captured and is transformed into the prison environment. Never be ashamed of being a prisoner of Jesus Christ, **Romans 1:16** – For I am not ashamed of the gospel of Christ: for it is the power of God unto salvation to everyone that believeth; to the Jew first, and also to the Greek. As a prisoner, you must bless the Lord at all times, **Psalm 34:1**, while you live and lift up your hands in His name. Agree with the devil, you are a prisoner; however, a prisoner of Jesus Christ. You are a prisoner that is not bond, but free in Christ Jesus, **John 8:36** – If the Son therefore shall make you free, ye shall be free indeed. You have been captured by the love of the Holy Ghost, **Romans 5:8** – And hope maketh not ashamed; because the love God is shed abroad in our hearts by the Holy Ghost which is given unto us. Your prison uniform is sewed in righteousness, holiness, covered with the Lord's grace and mercy. Jesus, the warden of your soul is amazing in all that He does for you in the Prison Gate. You are now free never to be put in bondage by any man or circumstance of life, **Galatians 4:9** – But now, after that ye have known God, how turn ye again to the weak and beggarly elements, whereunto ye desire again to be in bondage? You are free, **Galatians 5:1** – Stand fast therefore in the liberty wherewith Christ hath made us free, and be not entangled again with the yoke of bondage. Therefore, never let the devil make you a prisoner in your mind, heart, spirit or body. You are a prisoner of Jesus Christ, only, **II Timothy 2:9** – Wherein I suffer trouble, as an evildoer, even unto bonds; but the word of God is not bound. You are chained to Jesus by His love, and Jesus is linked to you because of your love for Him. Always remember, you are free in Jesus Christ, **John 8:36**. As you enter the Prison Gate you will hear the sounds of surrender from your mind, body and soul to the warden, Jesus Christ. You are not ashamed that you are a prisoner of Jesus Christ. Every prisoner has a cell. Most prison cells are 6 by 8 feet in size with bars on the outside. Your prison cell is very spacious and with no bars. You are free in Christ Jesus. You have resolved in your mind and now have the mind of Christ and undertook the position of righteousness in all that you say or do. You have committed to the rules of engagement, the Bible, and there are no bars to keep you in, remember you are free. You now know and believe that the Lord has your best interest at hand as a prisoner in His prison yard. In the Lord's prison yard, you will be able to exercise and flex your spiritual muscles. Your spiritual tools, discernment, will be sharpened to do the will of God in the Prison Gate. Natural prisoners are given numbers; not names but a number to be identified with. Spiritually, you can relate to a number to but that number is in relationship to the Word of God. It must be the number one which shows that you believe in One God that you have heard about, **Deuteronomy 6:4** – Hear, O Israel, the Lord our God is one Lord. Maybe you decided to walk with the number two, you and Jesus, **Amos 3:3** – Can two walk together, except they be agreed? Or maybe you will be given the number 3 expressing you are walking with God the Father, God the Son and God the Holy Ghost and all three have become real to you in the prison yard. In the prison yard, an open space to exercise and loosen up with other prisoners in conversation, you carry 66 books around with you and the books are hid in your heart. Why 66? There are sixty-six books in the Bible, 39 in Old Testament and 27 in the New Testament that you carry in your heart because of the a life sentence and must mediate on the Word of God day and night, **Joshua 1:8** – This book of the law shall not depart out of thy mouth; but thou shalt mediate therein day and night, that thou mayest observe to do according to all that is written therein: for thou shalt make thy way prosperous, and then thou shalt have good success. As a prisoner of Jesus, you will not fail because of His Word. You know that the Word of God must never depart from you, **Proverbs 4:21-22** – Let them not depart from thine eyes; keep them in the midst of thine heart. For they are life unto those that find them, and health to all their flesh. When satan comes and tells you not to read the Word of God, tell him that you are prisoner of Jesus Christ and you belong to Jesus. Prison food is good, bread alone for the prisoner of Jesus Christ, **Deuteronomy 8:3** – And he humbled thee, and suffered thee to hunger, and fed thee with manna, which thou knewest not, neither did thy fathers know; that he might make thee know that man doth not live by bread only, but by every word that proceedeth out of the mouth of the Lord doth man live. The prison yard will humble you but the Word of God will sustain you. There will be times when you will feel that you need to break out of the prison, keep your feet. When the devil comes and tries to break you out, you tell the devil, "Jesus has the keys." When you step into the Prison Gate, the first thing you must do is strip from everything that is not like the Lord. You must take off everything that will hinder your righteous talk and walk with the Lord. Satan will speak into your mind and you might agree that you should not be here and want to plan your escape, **Hebrews 2:3**. You will have to get adjusted; however, joy will come as you proceed day by day. After you strip, you are strip searched. The Spirit of God wants you to get rid of all hidden agendas. You are in the Prison Gate to learn to be kept by God. God gives you everything in life, food, shelter, and your stability for your life in God. You will learn the elements of submission and yielding to the will of God for your life. The Prison Gate attire is the garment of righteousness. The garment of the flesh is no longer an issue in your life because of the garment of righteousness, **Roman 10:3**. You begin to recognize the authority of God over your life, **Roman 13:1**. Paul was a prisoner of Rome but he was more a prisoner of Jesus Christ, **Ephesians 3:1**. Your life as a prisoner of Jesus Christ must be a life of discipline that can only be found in the Word of God. Settle in and let's go through the Prison Gate. You will wake up to see another day at God's appointed time. You will realize that it was not the alarm clock or someone shaking you, you will give God the praise for seeing another day. You will have a time of leisure prayer with the Lord, thanking him that you live, move and have your being because of the Lord, **Acts 17:28**. Throughout the day, you will be given breakfast, lunch, and dinner by the Word of God, **Matthew 4:4** or called to a day of fasting, **Isaiah 58:6**. Whatever, you will be content, **I Timothy 6:6**. You may have leisure time with other prisoners, fellow laborers in the Gospel of Jesus Christ. Get involved with other prisoners to become helpers one to another, **I Thessalonians 5:11**. You may meet others in prayer or Bible study. There will always be a time for work in the Prison Gate. The best job is encouraging other prisoners to hold on to their faith. There is always a job to do for your Lord, **Colossians 3:23** – And whatsoever ye do, do it heartily, as for the Lord, and not unto man. There is never a time for idleness, ask Jesus. Some days in the Prison Gate are some good and some bad. You will need encouraging some days. You must look to someone who can give you strength on bad days, i.e., a pastor, evangelist, teacher of the Word of God, prophet or an apostle. They are in the Prison Gate to obtain these titles that only the Lord can give them, **Ephesians 4:11**, for your spiritual edification. Time for retiring and you may want a snack but there is no snack but the Word of God, **Matthew 4:4**, every word of God. You reflect with the Word of God as your guide of your first day in the Prison Gate. Your whole being will be filled with enjoyment that you have helped someone else along this narrow way because you are a prisoner of Jesus Christ. In the Prison Gate there are no bars on your cell because you are free **John 8:36**. There is no death roll; but a life sentence because you have newness of life that you found in Christ Jesus, **II Corinthians 5:17**. In the Prison Gate, you don't have to watch your back because you are covered by the Blood of Jesus and the words of your testimony, **Revelation 12:11**. You can be kept in maximum, medium or minimum security in God. Some in the church today just want to be kept in minimum or medium security when they should strive to be kept in maximum security. Maximum security prisoner is a true threat to the devil. Jesus was a maximum security prisoner sent by God. Jesus said and accomplished what God sent Him to do for mankind. In maximum security, you cannot escape if you try because of the love of God. Maximum security you will have to go over a high wall and that is the Lord. Jesus is so high, you can't go over Him and He is so wide, you can't go around Him. This is why you must come in through the Door, Jesus, of the Prison Gate, **John 10:7**. In the Prison Gate, go to permanent lockdown in Christ Jesus because you are fully persuaded and you can't escape even when you want to breakout, **II Timothy 1:12**. You will begin to serve your time in the Prison Gate in super maximum security with a fully made up mind to serve the Lord and have accepted to serve the full sentence until the day you die. Then you will be able to say like Paul said, "I have fought a good fight, I have finished my course, and I have kept the faith", **II Timothy 4:7**. You will enjoy your time spent in the yard of Prison Gate because you are free in the Lord. Remember the reward at the end of your stay in the Prison Gate is a crown of righteousness which the Lord will give to you on that day, **II Timothy 4:8**. People will try to derogate your relationship with the Lord. Remain always a prisoner of Jesus and not a prisoner of people. Stay faithful over a few things and the Lord will make you ruler over many in the East Gate.

11

The East Gate – Nehemiah 3:29

The East Gate is reached by the ultimate mature Saint of God. In the East Gate you must dwell in that secret place, **Psalms 91** – He that dwelleth in the secret place of the most High shall abide under the shadow of the Almighty. You will be like Moses, the Lord will set you on the cleft of the rock and you will see the glory of the Lord manifested in your life, **Exodus 33:22**. This secret place in God is where the devil cannot come and disturb your peace and joy because you have become the apple of the Lord's eye, **Psalm 17:8**. You put in remembrance the prior gates and know that God brought you to the East Gate because He has been your dwelling place since accepting Him as your Savior. In the time of trouble, in each gate, the Lord hid you in the times of trouble. You are truly blessed in the East Gate because the Lord has walked this way before you, **Ezekiel 44:2** – Then said the Lord unto me; This gate shall be shut, it shall not be opened, and no man shall enter in by it; because the Lord, the God of Israel, hath entered in by it, therefore it shall be shut. The East Gate experience comes to a fully mature Christian with a made up mind and a fixed heart to serve the Lord until called home or meets the Lord in the air, **I Thessalonians 4:17** – Then we which are alive and remain shall be caught up together with him in the clouds, to meet the Lord in the air: and so shall be ever be with the Lord. This is why it is so important to stay "alive" in Christ Jesus and never be canal minded, stiff necked or asleep concerning the Word of God. Every morning you are expecting the Lord to come at any time and you have packed yourself in righteousness and you are ready to go at His appearance. You know that one morning or it might be evening, you will be raptured out of this world because you have come to the conclusion that this world is not your home, **I Peter 2:11**, that you have a better home in the heavens where Jesus abides and you have put your treasures in heaven and not on this earth, **Matthew 6:19-20**. You look at yourself in the East Gate and you are please at what you see and you have the confidence that the Lord is pleased too. You have grown in the Lord by His Word and the experiences of the gates of life have left you with just a wait in your heart on the Lord, **Psalm 27:14** – Wait on the Lord: be of good courage, and he shall strengthen thine heart: wait, I say, on the Lord. The expectation is the return of the Lord to invite you into the East Gate through life on this earth, through death or rapture. You have no choice in the matter, as long as you are accepted to pass through the East Gate. The conclusion of the whole matter of the Gates is that the East Gate, where the Lord walked, **Ezekiel 44:1-4**, and this East Gate is shut. However, the East Gate can be and will be opened to you when you live according to the Word of God. The requirements are to be "Holy" unto the Lord and "Sanctified" in the Word of God possessing the attributes of the

Lord, **Acts 10:38** – How God anointed Jesus of Nazareth with the Holy Ghost and with power: who went about doing good, and healing all that were oppressed of the devil; for God was with him. To enter the East Gate, you must be anointed by the Holy Ghost and set apart for the Master's use to triumph over whatever the challenge may be. The East Gate is shut because nothing goes in that does not have the attributes of Jesus and what Jesus stands for, "Holiness." The East Gate is accredited to only Jesus. Everything in the East Gate is accredited to the Glory of God. The star in the East showed where Jesus was born and the wise men saw the star and wanted to go and worship Him, **Matthew 2:2**. To enter into the glory of the Lord, you must worship Him; then you must see Jesus for Who He is and What He is, the Son of the Living God. Jesus will become the bright and the morning star in all that is around you, **Revelations 22:16** - ....I am the root and the offspring of David, and the bright and morning star, and all you can say is "Amen" with your whole heart. Amen means that it is settled and has been established in your heart. Whenever the hindrances in your life has been taken away, only after this, you will be able to enter into the East Gate, **Isaiah 6:1** – In the year that king Uzziah died I saw also the Lord sitting upon a throne, high and lifted up, and his train filled the temple. Everything that you counted as more worthy in your life to praise more than God, you have done away with that foolishness. Today is the day to see the glory of God and this is only when you enter the East Gate. Jesus has become your Savior, your friend and now He reveals Himself as the Holy One of God in His Glory high and lifted up. The East Gate can be a scary place but it must be a place where you must keep the utmost respect and reverence for

God. The East Gate is more than paramount and better than HD in a Christian's life, to see the glory of God. Moses asked to see the glory of God, **Exodus 33:18** – And he said, I beseech thee, shew me thy glory. The Lord granted Moses his petition. He showed Moses his goodness but not His face because no man can see God's face and live. The East Gate represents the power of God. This is why to enter into the East Gate you must have the Word of God in your heart, **Hebrews 4:12** – For the Word of God is quick, and powerful, and sharper than any two-edged sword, piercing even to the dividing asunder of soul and spirit, and of the joints and marrow, and is a discerner of the thoughts and intents of the heart. The Word of God gives you the experience of God's power in your life. The church today is calling it "being anointed." Has the true anointing been represented in an individual because they can sing or perform? This is not the true anointing. The true anointing is mentioned in **Luke 4:18-19** – The Spirit of the Lord is upon me, because he hath anointed me to preach the gospel to the poor; he hath sent me to heal the brokenhearted, to preach deliverance to the captives, and recovering of sight to the blind, to set at liberty them that are bruised, and to preach the acceptable year of the Lord. The Lord takes you into His anointing to experience the glory of God to be manifested in your life. The best part of the East Gate is that you will see Jesus for who He is in your life. Throughout all the other gates, you see Jesus in what He can do in your life. You recognize how Jesus can help you and give you what you need to sustain yourself in this Christian walk. However now, you will experience Jesus for Who He is because you will become like Him, **I John 3:2** – Beloved, now are we the sons of God, and doth not yet appear what we shall be: but we know that, when he shall appear, we shall be like him: for we shall see him as he is. When you look at the stars at night, they will shine differently when you look at them because you will think of Jesus, the Bright and Morning Star, **Revelation 21:16**. Who knows, you may be looking at the same star that shined on the night of Jesus' birth and guided the wise men to His manager, **Matthew 2:9**. In the elite part of the East Gate, you learn to acknowledge the Lord in all your ways**, Proverbs 3:5** – Trust in the Lord with all thine heart; and lean not unto thine own understanding. In all thy ways acknowledge him, and he shall direct thy paths. Before reaching the East Gate your thoughts became the Lord's thoughts and His ways became your ways and you allowed the Lord to direct your footsteps. You have begun to honor the Lord with your whole being, **Psalms 86:12** – I will praise thee, O Lord my God, and with all my heart: and I will glorify thy name for evermore. You know that the Lord is leading and guiding you to the privileged position in Himself, His glory in the East Gate. Just like Solomon shows the glory of the Lord in God's house that Solomon built, you will see the same glory in your home, **II Chronicles 7:1 –** Now when Solomon had made an end of praying, the fire came down from heaven, and consumed the burnt-offering and the sacrifices; and the glory of the Lord filled the house. When you worship and pray in your home the glory of the Lord has a right to be there. You worship in your home by magnifying the Lord in your life style the glory of the Lord will take over your whole being. There is no fussing or cussing in your home only holy conversations and manner of lifestyle, the glory of the Lord will be there. Allow gospel music edify you and enlighten the atmosphere with the presence of the Lord. You set the tone and the devil will flee and the Holy Ghost will come in and make its abode. As soon as Solomon ended praying, the glory of the Lord filled the temple. You must have the knowledge and the wisdom of God as you diligently seek His face to experience the glory of God here on this earth. Paul experienced the glory of God so much that it was expedient for him to talk about it, **II Corinthians 12:2**. Today, you must talk about the soon coming of your Lord and Savior and He is coming in His glory, **Mark 13:26** – And then shall they see the Son of man coming in the clouds with great power and glory. You must experience the East Gate now to truly appreciate the Lord's appearance when He returns back to the earth. The Lord is here with you now and will return to receive you unto Himself. The signs of the times are here, especially the perilous times, **II Timothy 3:1**. These are dangerous times that vex the souls of mankind. You will need the Shekhinah glory of the Lord everywhere you go in the latter days. In your home, make your house, God's house, with dedication unto Him and your house will become His dwelling place. In your church, make your church God's tabernacle, where the divine presence of the Lord dwells, **Psalms 15:1-5** – Lord, who shall abide in thy tabernacle? Who shall dwell in thy holy hill? Who can enter into the East Gate? Are you one that walks uprightly, works righteousness and speak truth in your heart? Is your tongue in control and speaks no evil to your neighbor or take up a reproach against your neighbor? Do you hate evil and honor them that fear the Lord? If the check list has nothing but "Yes, Lord, Yes", then joy bells are ringing in your soul. You can sing the highest praise, "Hallelujah", thanking God for His power each and every day.

Jesus has become King of kings and Lord of lord in your life. What a beautiful picture when the Lord looks at you, the apple of His eyes. He is the Lord above. In our God come salvation and glory, honor, dominion and power to the Lord above because you have found your God to be Wonderful, Counsellor, the mighty God, The Everlasting Father, the Prince of Peace, and now in the East Gate you have been introduced to a child that became the Son that was given, **Isaiah 9:6** - For unto us a child is born, unto us a son is given….and His Name is Jesus of the East Gate. You must recognize Jesus as the power of all things with no exception, **John 1:3** – All things were made by him; and without him was not anything made that was made. You must know it is only Jesus who took you through the prior gate to truly appreciate the East Gate. Nehemiah repairers did not have to repair the East Gate. Why? Nothing is broken down in heaven and let it be as on earth as it is in heaven. Whatever is in heaven shall be like wise on this earth. East Gate represents Jesus and anything in Jesus need not be repaired. Jesus is the repairer of the breach. Jesus is fullness of the God head, **Colossians 2:9-10** – For in him dwelleth all the fullness of the Godhead bodily. And ye are complete in him, which is the head of all principality and power. We have the God the Father, God the Son and God the Holy Ghost who is the head of all principality and power. When you see Jesus in everything you do and say, just say "Amen." The presence of the Lord is in the East Gate. There is no denunciation and no apprehension in the East Gate because the Lord has walked this way before you. There are blessings and fullness of joy in the East Gate which represents the glory of the Lord and the dwelling place of the Lord, **Ezekiel 44:1-4** – Then he brought me back the way of the gate of the outward sanctuary which looketh toward the east: and it was shut. Then said the Lord unto me; This gate shall be shut, it shall not be opened, and no man shall enter in by it; because the Lord, the God of Israel, hath entered in by it, therefore it shall be shut. It is for the prince; the prince, he shall sit in it to eat bread before the Lord; he shall enter by the way of the porch of that gate, and shall go out by the way of the same. Then brought me the way of the north gate before the house: and I looked, and behold, the glory of the Lord filled the house of the Lord and I fell upon my face. In the East Gate, you will lay upon your face at times in the presence of the Lord. The more you acknowledge the Lord in all your ways, you will see Jesus as Isaiah saw Him, high and lifted up, **Isaiah 6:1**. In the dwelling place of the Lord, there is the glory of the Lord. At all times in the East Gate you must reverence God and the very presence of God. This is why pure worship, bowing before the Lord, acknowledging the presence of God and reverence to His Holy Name must never leave the church. The entertainment elements in the church have taken the place of pure worship. All church must wait for the presence of the Lord to come and come to the conclusion, "Without the Lord, I can do nothing", **John 15:5** -....for without me ye can do nothing and with God all Things are Possible", **Matthew 19:26** – But Jesus beheld them, and said unto them, with men this is impossible, but with God all things are possible, in the presence of the Lord. You will see diseases healed, blinded eyes open and even the dead come back to life again. Stay in the tabernacle of the Lord and meet the criteria to stay there, The question was asked, **Psalm 15:1-5**, Lord, who shall abide in thy tabernacle and who shall dwell in thy holy hill? Keep the glory cloud of the Lord over you by day and night, **Exodus 24:16-18** – And the glory of the Lord abode upon mount Sinai, and the cloud covered it six days: and the seventh day he called unto Moses out of the mist of the cloud. And the sight of the glory of the Lord was like a devouring fire on the top of the mount in the eyes of the children of Israel. Keep the Sabbath, **Exodus 20:8** – Remember the Sabbath day, to keep it holy. Then the presence of the Lord will make its presence known in the congregation, it is like fire, especially when the preached Word of God is spoken, **Luke 24:32** - And they said one to another, Did not our heart burn within us, while he talked with us by the way, and while he opened to us the scriptures? Remember, the devouring fire was on the top of the mount. So, you must see God, keep looking up, **Psalms 121:1** – I will lift up mine eyes unto the hills, from whence cometh my help. Remember this is an individual way, I will. Remember to enter into the Lord's gate always in the right frame of mind and spirit, **Psalms 100:4** –Enter into his gates with thanksgiving, and into his courts with praise: be thankful unto him, and bless his name. Do away with foolishness and unforgiveness; they have no position in God presence. When you enter into the presence of the Lord, you are coming into the presence of the full deity of Christ, **Colossians 2:9** – For in him dwelleth all the fullness of the godhead bodily. You are standing before God the Father, God the Son and God the Holy Ghost and all three are one, **Deuteronomy 6:4** – Hear, O Israel: The Lord our God is one Lord. The reverence for the God-head is diminishing from the church in prayer and worship service and in general the respect that is due God's holy Name. Many do not understand when you pray, you pray to all three at the same time.

Pray to God to reference His Name, **Matthew 6:9** – After this manner therefore pray ye: Our Father which art in heaven, Hallowed be thy name. This prayer honors God as your Father in heaven. Pray to Jesus to ask, **Matthew 14:13** – And whatsoever ye shall ask me in my name, that will I do that the Father may be glorified in the Son. Jesus goes to the Father. The Holy Ghost is the Spirit of God Who comforts you and leads you into all truths, **John 16:13** – Howbeit when he, the Spirit of truth, is come, he will guide you into all truth: for he shall not speak of himself: but whatsoever he shall hear, that shall he speak: and he will show you things to come. This shows any believer one thing, God's name should never be taken in vain, **Exodus 20:7** – Thou shalt not take the name of the Lord thy God in vain: for the Lord will not hold him guiltless that taketh his name in vain and the Holy Ghost is not an "it" but a Comforter, **John 15:26** – But when the Comforter is come, whom I will send unto you from the Father, even the Spirit of truth, which proceeded from the Father, he shall testify of me. At the East Gate when you just think about this God, the True and Living God, who made the heaven and the earth, that is enough to give God, His Son Jesus Christ and His Power, the Holy Ghost all what is due His Name. Jesus is God's Son, Emanuel, meaning God with us, **Matthew 1:23** – Behold, a virgin shall be with child, and shall bring forth a son, and they shall call his name Immanuel, which being interpreted is, God with us. Father, all the church can do right now is asking God through His Son, Jesus Christ, by the power of the Holy Ghost, forgiving us when we do reverence Your Name. As a remembrance, in the East Gate you will come to the conclusion, and hear, church, our God is One God, **Mark 12:29-30** – And Jesus answered him, The first of all the commandments is, Hear, O Israel; the Lord our God is one Lord: and Thou shalt love the Lord thy God with all thy heart and with all thy soul;, and with all thy mind, and with all thy strength: this is the first commandment. This sounds like a requirement for coming into the East Gate. The church world must be very careful how they enter into the presence of the Lord, **Psalm 132:7** – We will go into his tabernacles: we will worship at his footstool. When you enter into the East Gate, you come for no other reason but to worship God. If you are under a pastor or a church that does not worship the Lord with the clapping of hands, **Psalm 47**:1 – O Clap your hands, all ye people; shout unto God with the voice of triumph because the floods clap their hands…**Psalm 98:8** or lifting up the voice of praise unto the Lord, you are in a church that will never reach the East Gate. You must make a joyful noise unto the Lord, **Psalms 98:4** - Make a joyful noise unto the Lord, all the earth: make a loud noise, and rejoice, and sing praise. You do not come to church to be entertained. We serve the Mighty, Powerful God, Who made the heavens and the earth. The heaven is God's throne and the earth is his footstool, **Isaiah 66:1** – Thus saith the Lord, the heaven is my throne, and the earth is my footstool: where is the house that ye build unto me? And where is the place of my rest? Jesus is the Rock that the church is built upon, **Matthew 16:18**. He is over the church and loves the church so much that He gave His life for you. As you respect God and respect the fellow sheep in His pasture we all will obtain passage to the East Gate. We all must come to the East Gate in the same frame of mind that has been sanctified. How do we get to the East Gate? The only answer is by faith. You must have the type of faith that pleases God, **Hebrews 11:6** – But without faith it is impossible to please him: for he that cometh to God must believe that he is, and that he is a rewarder of them that diligently seek him. If we stand on our tippy toes, we cannot reach heaven but by faith we can reach the East Gate the dwelling place of God, **Isaiah 55:8-9** – For my thoughts are not your thoughts, neither are your ways my ways, saith the Lord. For as the heavens are higher than the earth, so are my ways higher than your ways, and my thoughts than your thoughts. Don't try to figure it out, just believe that God wants you to come to the East Gate. However, with confidence, devotion and faithfulness in the Word of God we can obtain the mind of God to enter into the East Gate. In the presence of the Lord, standing or sitting, is where you want to be, **Psalm 16:11** – Thou wilt shew me the path of life: in the presence is fullness of joy; at thy right hand there are pleasures for evermore. Each child of God should endeavor to have their own experience in the presence of the Lord. Some times as you watch people singing and praising God, get this experience for yourself. The joy of the Lord will have you crying one moment and shouting for joy the next moment. Paul knew about the East Gate and being in the presence of the Lord. The East Gate will reveal the mysteries of God to His man or woman of God. You will have an experience and some things you will be unable to tell anyone, **II Corinthians 12:1-4** – **Vs 1** - It is not expedient for me doubtless to glory. I will come to visions and revelations of the Lord. Paul had a personal experience on the Road to Damascus when He met the Lord. To know the Lord is to have an intimate relationship for you to get dreams and visions from the Lord, **Joel 2:28** – And it shall come to pass afterward, that I will pour out my spirit upon all flesh: and your sons and hour daughters shall prophesy, your old men shall dream dreams, your young men shall see visions. All must have their own private walk with the Lord for visions and revelations of the Lord. **Vs 2** - I knew a man in Christ above fourteen years ago, (whether in the body, I cannot tell; or whether out of the body, I cannot tell: God knoweth;) such a one caught up to the third heaven. Paul was talking about himself. After Paul's conversion, he was truly "in" Christ Jesus, **II Corinthians 5:17** – Therefore if any man be in Christ, he is a new creature: old things are passed away; behold, all things are become new, what an experience. Paul was caught up in the third heave. The first heaven is the earth's atmosphere. Look up and you can see it, the sky which contains the clouds and beautiful blue or gray where the rain will fall sometimes. The second heaven is the cosmos, stars, moon, and sun. Man calls this the "Outer Limit" even where man fears to tread. The third heaven is God's dwelling place, **Deuteronomy 10:14** – Behold, the heaven and the heaven of heavens is the Lord's thy God, the earth also, with all that therein is. **Vs 4** – How that he was caught up into paradise, and heard unspeakable words, which it is not lawful for a man to utter. The heavenly language Paul heard was not allowed to man to speak. Just like we will have a new name in heaven; we will have a new language in heaven. `The East is very special direction for the Saint of God with true meaning pertaining to our Lord and Savior. **Matthew 2:1-2** – Now when Jesus was born in Bethlehem of Judea in the days of Herod the king, behold, there were wise men from the east to Jerusalem, Saying, where is he that is born King of the Jews? For we have seen his star in the east, and are come to worship him. The Wise men came from the

East and saw the star in the East signifying that the King of the Jews was born. Many religions pray facing the east. We pray facing all directions, knowing that God is everywhere, because you know that God is omnipresent. God is everywhere in your space and universe. Before you enter into the East Gate, you must in the East Gate acknowledge the glory of God, **Psalm 19:1** – The heavens are telling of the glory of God. And their expanse is declaring the work of His hands. The glory of the Lord is in the East Gate. When you come near the East Gate, the senses of awesomeness most come over you from the top of your head to the soles of your feet. You are in the presence of the True and Living God, the Lord. Each time you open up your Bible, you are in the East Gate awaiting revelation knowledge that only comes from the Lord, **John 1:14** – And the Word was made flesh, and dwelt among us, and we beheld his glory, the glory as of the only begotten of the Father, full of grace and truth. Queen Elizabeth, President Obama or any one that sits in the position of authority is not like the authority in the East Gate, **Hebrews 1:3** – And He is the radiance of His glory and the exact representation of his nature, and upholds all things by the word of his power. When He had made purification of sins, He sat down at the Right Hand of the Majesty on high. It is an awesome majesty because Jesus came, died, and rose again and sitting on the right Hand of God making intercession for you as you enter into the East Gate. The fear of the Lord, which is the beginning of wisdom, must be presented within your being when entering into the East Gate. In the East Gate the Lord's name is to be honored, **Deuteronomy 28:58** – If you are not careful to observe all the words of this law which are written in this book, to fear this honored and awesome name, the Lord your God. Blessed the Lord, O my soul and all that is within me, bless His Holy Name, **Job 37:22** - ...around God is awesome majesty. God has clothed Himself with splendor and majesty, **Psalm 145:5**. The East Gate is not a gate to play the fool. In fact, a fool will never get into the East Gate, **Psalm 14:1** – A fool has said in his heart, there is no God. God's business is conducted in the East Gate. In prophecy, the Lord is going to return in the East, **Ezekiel 44:1** – Then he brought me back the way of the gate of the outward sanctuary which looked toward the east; and it was shut. So many in the church today cannot truly say that they have come into the East Gate, we have to examine our worship in the house of God. You cannot be rebellious and enter into the East Gate, **Ezekiel 44:5-8** – And the Lord said unto me, Son of man, mark well, and behold with thine eyes, and hear with thine ears all that I say unto thee concerning all the ordinances of the house of the Lord, and all the laws thereof; and mark well the entering in the house, with every going forth of the sanctuary. Are the church leaders, pastors, teachers, evangelists, prophets and apostles, truly listening to the Lord's Voice today? We have to ask ourselves before we can get to the East Gate, have we become hearers and not doers of the Word of God, **James 1:22** – But be ye doers of the word, and not hearers only, deceiving your own selves. We can't hear only parts of the Bible but we must listen to the entire Bible. You must hear and have the Word of God in action in your life. You are only deceiving yourself and your worship will stink in the nostrils of God. You must worship the Lord in spirit and in truth. You will only offer the Lord strange fire to the Lord in your worship, **Leviticus 10:1-2** – And Nadab and Abihu, the sons of Aaron, took either of them his censer and put fire therein, and put incense thereon, and offered strange fire before the Lord, which he commanded them not. And there went out fire from the Lord, and devoured them, and they died before the Lord. In the East Gate, God will deal with strange worship and praise in His sanctuary. We have to mindful of how we enter into the House of God. We must be mindful how we handle the Word of God, which represents God's Son, Jesus. We also must be mindful of the fire we present to God in worship. Is the worship from the heart and pure? Is the worship holy? Or, is it stranger fire? Strange fire not authorized in the East Gate. Worldliness in the East Gate is unacceptable, **Leviticus 10:9-10** – Do not drink wine nor strong drink....and that ye may put difference between holy and unholy, and between unclean and clean. To enter into the East Gate, you must be sanctified, from the pulpit to the congregation, **Leviticus 10:3** – Then Moses said unto Aaron, This is it that the Lord spoke, saying, I will be sanctified in them that come nigh me, and before all the people I will be glorified. And Aaron held his peace. You must ensure that you are reverencing the Lord in His worship when entering and departing the Lord's sanctuary. Foolish talk of yesterday is dropped at the door. Always remember, you are in the presence of the True and Living God. One of the ordinances of the Lord is the Lord's Supper, **II Corinthians 11:28-30** – Wherefore whosoever shall eat this bread, and drink this cup of the Lord, unworthily, shall be guilty of the body and blood of the Lord. But let a man examine himself, and so let him eat of that bread, and drink of that cut. For he that eateth and drinketh unworthily, eateth and drinketh damnation to himself, not discerning the Lord's body. For this cause many are weak and sickly among you, and many sleep. Let us examine ourselves with full repentance. The offering table is a part of worship also and we are robbing God, **Malachi 3:8** – Will a man rob God? Yet ye have robbed me. But ye say, Wherein have we robbed thee? In tithes and offering. Many in the church have been deceived and badly mistaken when they do not obey the Word of God. When you disobey the Word of God you fall into error and error will lead you down the path of sin. Giving your tithes and offering is a ministry of the church and it honors and worships God. The East Gate experience will make you glad when they said unto you, "Let us go into the house of the Lord", **Psalm 122:1** – I was glad when they said unto me, Let us go into the house of the Lord. Why? In the presence of the Lord, there is fullness of joy - **Psalm 16:11** – Thou wilt shew me the path of life: in thy presence is fullness of joy; at thy right hand there are pleasures for evermore and liberty, **II Corinthians 3:17** – Now the Lord is that Spirit: and where the spirit of the Lord is, there is liberty. You must be successful in the prior Gates to reach the East Gate. In the East Gate all foolish acts in word or deed is dropped left in the Dung Gate. A pure and humble heart is always with you in the East Gate because of your reverence in prayer and worship for the Lord. With this continued awe, you are advancing toward the Final Gate. The Lord wants His people to come into His courts with thanksgiving and into His house with praise because He inhabits the praises of His people, **Psalm 22:3** – But thou art holy, O thou that inhabitest the praises of Israel. The church must know and realize they serve an awesome God, **I Chronicles 16:25** – For great is the Lord, and greatly to be praised: he also is to be feared above all gods. The Lord is worthy to be praised; therefore, you must be worthy to enter into the East Gate and the Lord is the only One who can make you worthy. You are completely sold out to living for the Lord. Your mind is made up and your heart is completely fixed to walk with the Lord and to talk to the Lord, **Mark 12:30** – And thou shalt love the Lord thy God with all thy heart, and with all thy soul, and with all thy mind, and with all thy strength: this is the first commandment. In the East Gate, all aspects of church service will become truly real to you from the opening prayer of submission because you are in the presence of the True and Living God to the benediction, **Numbers 6:24-26** – The Lord bless thee, and keep thee. The Lord make his face shine upon thee, and be gracious unto thee: The Lord lift up his countenance upon thee, and give thee peace. When it is time to give your tithes and offerings, you will freely give because you have freely received. The best part of the service you will know it is not the choir but the sermon, the Word of God, **II Timothy 3:16** – All scriptures is given by inspiration of God, and is profitable for doctrine, for reproof, for correction, for instruction in righteousness. When the invitation is given, the altar call, you are not looking around but in the East Gate you are praying for those that need prayer and those that have come to accept the Lord into their lives. Many in the church will never experience the East Gate because their worship to God is out of order. They will be on the outside looking in and wondering why you are so happy and strong in the Lord. You don't have to explain nothing to anyone; you just keep coming closer and closer to your God and your Creator. Never let anyone in the church or the circular world tell you "that it doesn't take all that." What is all that? You that you don't have to go to church pray or read the Bible. The service services become so real to you that you cry during Communion. You examine yourself each time, **I Corinthians 11:25** – But let a man examine himself, and so let him eat of the bread, and drink of that cup. At the communion table you have found unity with Christ and in the resurrection of your soul because of Jesus. At the communion table you have taken part of Jesus death, burial, and resurrection and you know that you can never take the communion reluctantly. God know your heart is a very popular saying among the lukewarm and carnal people in the church today. They will never experience or reach the East Gate. The power of God will never be manifested in their lives. Continue to search for the Lord with your whole heart and your will find Him, **Jeremiah 29:13** – And ye shall seek me, and find me, when ye shall search for me with all your heart and you will find the Lord in the East Gate waiting for you to show you wonderful things, **Jeremiah 33:13** – Call unto me, and I will answer thee, and shew thee great and mighty things, which thou knows not. Final note, never forget, "Only the pure in heart shall see God, **Matthew 5:8**. The proclamation is the "Whole Truth" of the "Whole Matter" in Christ Jesus is found in the East Gate. You must live like you know the whole truth and you will not let nothing separate you from the Love of Jesus, **Romans 8:35-39** – Who shall separate us from the love of Christ? Shall tribulation, or distress, or persecution, or famine, or nakedness, or peril, or sword? As it is written, for thy sake we are killed all the day long; we are accounted as sheep for the slaughter. Nay, in all these things we are more than conquerors through him that loved us. For I am persuaded, that neither death, nor life, nor angels, nor principalities, nor powers, nor things present, nor things to come, nor height, nor depth, nor any other creature shall be able to separate us from the love of God, which is in Christ Jesus. Until that final day on this earth, you must stay completely persuaded and you will abide in the East Gate. This is your eternal beginning right here on earth in the East Gate to allow you to appreciate even the more your heavenly ending, right here on this earth. However, on that day, you will see Jesus and because of the East Gate experience, you will see Him in peace. You worshipped, honored and adore Him and one day He will call you by your name because you have kept His Hand in your hand. You have allowed the glory of the Lord to be manifested in your life. The One you have been waiting will come and take you home, **II Corinthians 5:8** – We are confident, I say, and of willing rather to be absent from the body, and to be present with the Lord. The wonders of the Lord are waiting for each one of His sheep from the Sheep Gate to the final conclusion to the East Gate. The Final Gate is in a whole different dimension. This Final Gate is an Eternal Gate in the Glory of the Lord in the atmosphere of eternity and not time.

The Final Gate – Revelation 21:12-13

The Final Gate takes you from earth to glory right here on earth to reach the heavenly atmosphere in your spiritual walk with the Lord. This final gate has a great reward waiting for you because you kept the faith and confidence in the Lord, **Hebrews 10:35** – Cast not away your confidence, which hath great recompense of reward. Rather you are on a bed of affliction or in the best of health, one day you know that you are going where the wicked shall stop troubling and weary shall be at rest, **Job 3:17**. One day, you will be absent from this body with full benefits from the Lord of the East Gate, **II Corinthians 5:8** – We are confident, I say, and willing rather to be absent from the body, and to be present with the Lord. All because you presented your body a living sacrifice, holy and acceptable unto God, one day, you will reach the Final Gate. Changes will occur, **I Corinthians 15:53** – For the corruptible must put on incorruption, and this mortal must put on immortality. You will be changed from the natural to the spiritual in the twinkling of an eye. Yes, this is a mystery. This can happen in time at any moment. It may be morning, night or noon.

On that day, you will not perish, but have everlasting life. On the day of your birth, you had your "good morning"; however, on the day of your death, you will have your "good night". Just like the sun must come up; the sun must go down. Death was a sentence given to Adam, **Genesis 3:19** – In the sweat of thy face shalt thou eat bread, till thou return unto the ground; for out of it wast thou taken: for dust thou art, and unto dust shalt thou return. Eternal life was given to you from the God you served throughout your life on earth, **John 3:16** – For God so loved the world that He gave His only begotten Son that whosoever believeth in him should not perish, but have everlasting life. Death is not to be feared, just be confident and believe the Word of God that Jesus has gone away to prepare a place for you, **John 14:1-2** – Let not your heart be troubled: ye believe in God, believe also in me. In my Father's house are many mansions: if it were not so, I would have told you. I go to prepare a place for you. You are confident and know to be absent from the body is to be present with the Lord, **II Corinthians 5:8**. On that day, you will say within yourself, **I Corinthians 15:55-57** – ….death is swallowed up in victory. O death, where is thy sting? O grave, where is thy victory? The sting of death is sin; and the strength of sin is the law. But thanks be to God, which giveth us the victory through our Lord Jesus Christ. You know in whom you have believed and His name is Jesus. Death is an appointment that we all must keep. No one but God can make the appointment or cancel the appointment; however, man must keep the appointment once. It is appointed unto to man once to die and then the judgment, **Hebrews 9:27**. Than you will hear the Voice of the One in the East Gate speak to you to "Come" because you have been good and faithful, **Matthew 25:21; 23** – His lord said unto him, Well done; thou good and faithful servant: thou hast been faithful over a few things, I will make thee ruler over may things: enter thou into the joy of the lord; His lord said unto him, well done, good and faithful servant, thou hast been faithful over a few things, I will make thee ruler over many things: enter thou into the joy of the Lord. On that day, you will walk up to one of the twelve gates, **Revelation 21:12** – And had a wall great and high, and had twelve gates, and at the gates twelve angels, and names written thereon which are the names of the twelve tribes of the children of Israel. What direction will you go in and which gate will you go in, **Revelations 21:13** – On the east three gates; on the north three gates; on the south three gates, and on the west three gates? You can only imagine the magnificence on that day. You will not be able to use the word time because in eternity there is no time. Looking at the brilliance of the gates; which one will you go in? Will you select gate number "**One**" because you served the only One faithful God, **I Corinthians 8:6** – But to us there is but one God, the Father, of whom are all things, and we in him; and one Lord Jesus Christ, by whom are all things, and we by him? Will you pick gate number "**Two**" because you agreed with the words of Jesus and walked with Him from earth to glory, **Amos 3:3** – Can two walk together, except they be agreed? You agreed with the things of God throughout your experience in your earthly gates. Or did you decide to take gate number "**Three**" because you appreciated the three in One that helped you, God the Father, God the Son and God the Holy Ghost. Maybe you will elect gate number "**Four**" because of the blessings you found in your time, Mountain, Pacific, Central and Eastern Gate and appreciated the blessings from the Lord in your season, Summer, Winter, Spring or Fall, and you know that all these blessings came from the Lord, **Proverbs 10:22** – The blessing of the Lord, it make rich and addeth no sorrow to it. Looking at gate number "**Five**", you may remember all the grace, goodness, favor and mercy that was rendered to you throughout your live, **John 1:16** – And of his fullness have all we received, and grace for grace. During the time of trouble, the Lord's grace will be sufficient for you, **II Corinthians 12:9**. Seeing gate number "**Six**", your mind reflects back to your humble beginning in the Sheep Gate. The Lord began to form you in His Word and you began to walk in each gate with destiny. God made you in His image on the sixth day even before you were born, **Genesis 1:26** – And God said, Let us make man in our image, after our likeness and let them have dominion over the fish of the sea, and over the fowl of the air, and over the cattle, and over all the earth, and over every creeping thing that creepeth upon the earth. You are half way through the decision that only God can give you. Which gate will you stroll through? Gate number "**Seven**", the number of rest and completion. You found rest in the Valley Gate because you entered into the rest of God, **Hebrews 4:9** – There remaineth therefore a rest to the people of God. Just as God rest after creation; you will rest for an eternity. Maybe your choice will be gate number "**Eight**"; after all, this is eternity representing a new beginning in this present world. You are a new creation in God with a new walk and a new talk because of your salvation. Gate number "**Nine**", as you walk through what will it hold for you. You are beginning to truly feel complete in God because of the nine fruits of the Spirit that helped you reach your final destination, **Galatians 5:22-23** – But the fruit of the Spirit is love, joy, peace, longsuffering, gentleness, goodness, faith, meekness, temperance: against such there is no law. Gate number "**Ten**" awaits you. You hid the Word of God; His ten commandments, His statutes and His laws in your heart with complete acceptance. Gate number "**Eleven**" may be your decision because you escaped the judgment of the second death. While on earth going through the gates of life, you kept disorder and confusion out of your life and your name was found written in the Book of Life. Looking at the final gate, "**Twelve**", you think of what God's Son Jesus had given you in each earthly gate, power and authority over the works of satan. You have followed Jesus by the example of His twelve disciples. One day this process will help you reach the point to stand at one of the twelve heavenly gates. The power and the authority that God gave you through His Son Jesus Christ have allowed you to stand and give Him praise throughout eternity. Now, praise the Lord and let Him keep you in that secret place in Him while here on earth and He will take you to that special place somewhere around His throne in heaven eternally.

Conclusion

Genesis to Malachi – Matthew to Revelation

As you study the Word of God from the Old Testament to the New Testament, you will appreciate the Words of the Bible that shows the lives of those that passed through the same gates that you are passing through today, **Romans 15:4**. From **Genesis** to **Malachi**, the patriarchs of the Old Testament walked with the God that they could not see. They accepted everything at "faith value." By faith, they believed and journeyed on through these gates, **Genesis 4:6** - …then began men to call among the name of the Lord, which they could not see. Adam and Eve began the journey for you because Adam was the first man that God created in His image. Eve was the first woman, the mother of all living. They began to walk through the gates when they were cast from the Garden of Eden. **Hebrews 11** is the chapter of the New Testament that shows you that those mentioned in the Old Testament walked by faith. You began to walk through these various gates when you were casted out of the world of sin, washed, and forgiven of your sins by the Blood of Jesus. You will begin to give the Lord the more excellent sacrifice just like Abel and you will begin to walk like Enoch and please God. You will believe in the warning that is streaming throughout the world today and stay in the ark of safety which is Jesus Christ. Just like Noah did and he saved his whole family. Due to a promise from God, Abram and Sari journeyed through many gates. Enoch kept walking through his gates until the Lord took him and he was seen no more by man, only by God. Jacob's gates allowed him to wrestle with an angel. Due to the famine in the land, Joseph's gates allowed his family's lives to be spared by God provision. Moses, from Pharaoh's house, to killing a man, to the desert, his gates allowed him to see the promise land. Samson's gate allowed him to defeated more enemies in his death than in his life. Job journeyed through his gates to his healing, deliverance, to prosperity. From **Genesis to Malachi**, many of the patriarchs of the Bible walked through the same gates you walked through walking and talking to God. Throughout all of the gates, something got a hold of you and it was a journey from gate to gate by the leading of the Holy Ghost, the pure Holy Spirit of God. From **Genesis to Malachi**, many of the patriarchs of the Bible walked through the same gates you walked through walking and talking to God. From Matthew to Revelations, you have presented yourself to the Lord throughout all the gates of your life. No you have not seen Jesus but you have seen and recognized Him in His Word, the Bible. Jesus came down as the prefect sacrifice and you accepted the sacrifice of the Lamb of God that gave you your process to His eternal kingdom through the gates of **Nehemiah 3**. Just like Mary, you began to carry the Word of God and ponder things in your heart as you walked with the King of kings and the Lord of lords and His name is Jesus. You heard His Voice and became one His disciples and refused to be a Judas. You refused to a Peter and deny what Jesus has done in your life in each gate to the point you go through crucifixion after crucifixion in this sinful world because of your belief, **II Timothy 3:12** – Yea, and all that will live godly in Christ Jesus shall suffer persecution. You must believe God no matter what gate the Lord opened in your life. By faith keep forsaking the world and you will see that city of God that is not made by man's hands. Keep a good report through your faith in God and you will receive a crown of life that only the Lord will give you on that day. Endure through your gates, **James 1:12** – Blessed is the man that endureth temptation: for when he is tried, he shall receive the crown of life, which the Lord hath promised to them that love him. This day, no matter what gate you are in, know that Jesus is there and He is soon to come back for His Bride, the church, **Hebrews 10:35-39** – Cast not away therefore your confidence, which hath great recompense of reward. For ye have need of patience, that, after ye have done the will of God, ye might receive the promise. For yet a little while, and he that shall come will come, and will not tarry. Now the just shall live by faith: but if any man draws back, my soul shall have no pleasure in him. But we are not of them who draw back unto perdition; but of them that believe to the saving of the soul from the Sheep Gate to the Eternal Gate. Thank you Jesus.

About the Author

Born November 19, 1951, in a small steel town in Johnstown, Pa to a God reverencing family upbringing. She accepted the Lord into her heart at the age of 15 when she saw fire shoot around the sanctuary and the Lord got her attention. She went into the military and decided not to play with God and rode the waves of a backslider. However, she told the Lord, "I'll be back." The Lord ever left her and she came back to the Lord after hating the sin that drove her from her Father's house. She came back to the Lord at the age of 31 and has been working in God's vineyard from Sister in her church, to Teacher of the Gospel, to Evangelist speaker of the Word of God, to Pastor over the sheep of God. She is the pastor of Bethel of Truth Church in Glenside, Pennsylvania with the founding scripture, **John 17:17** – Sanctify them by thou truth, for thy word is truth. She is married to Oscar Washington, Sr., two children, Melinda and Oscar Jr., and one grandson, Diamond.